FAST FLUENCY

INTERNATIONAL COMMUNICATION SERIES

FAST FLUENCY

Communication in English
for the International Age

William Boletta

Logos International

Published by Logos International
Tokyo, Japan, and San Francisco, California
Copyright © 1991 by Logos International
First Published 1991
Second Printing with Corrections 1992
Third Printing 1992

ISBN 4-947561-01-7

Printed in Hong Kong

To my father,
JOHN L. BOLETTA
Thanks for that first trip to Cossitt Library.

Acknowledgments

This book could not have been produced without the talents of Yoshitsugu Nakamura of Logos International, who gave constant assistance with the concept, design, layout, execution, and production. His ideas, comments, and suggestions are reflected on literally every page.

Thanks to my colleague Robert Gray for his support and encouragement of my work, especially his sharing with me his considerable experience as a teacher of English as a foreign language and his ever-current knowledge of applied linguistics.

Special thanks to J. D. Larson and the crew at P. O. Plus in San Francisco, who kept the communications channels flowing between Tokyo and San Francisco, often going to great lengths to assure that we had the requisite software and hardware necessary to carry out the Fast Fluency project. Without their help, this book would never have seen the light of day on either side of the Pacific.

While the above friends, colleagues, and associates deserve credit for their support and assistance, any shortcomings the book might have are solely the responsibility of the author.

Finally, I would like to thank my students over several years, particularly those in my Conversational English classes at Senshu University and Waseda University in Tokyo. Their interests, needs, and ambitions gave me an audience to write for.

W. B.

Contents

To
The Student

L ANGUAGE IS A TOOL. Like all tools, it has many uses, but it is not worth very much by itself. We use language to express thoughts or feelings. Grammar and words alone are not as important as the content of what you say. In fact, without content and meaning, language would be useless.

Language, then, is a way to communicate what you need, want, think, or feel. This is true of all languages, not only English. Your native language and English are very similar. Both are used to communicate with other human beings. This is true of all languages in all countries.

How can I learn to speak English?

English is not a mystery or secret. Anybody can learn it as a second language, and millions of people do every year, but if you want to learn to speak English, you must be willing to do two things: Make mistakes and take chances.

When you speak English, you will make some mistakes because nobody can start speaking a foreign language perfectly from the start. If you wait until you know all the words and forms perfectly, you will never be able to speak English. So start now, wherever you are in your English studies, and speak the best way you can. You can learn new words and better grammar later, but if you don't start talking now, you will never improve.

This is why it is important to take chances. If you wait until you are sure that everything you say will be perfect, you will wait a long time. *Maybe forever!* Don't be afraid to say what you want to—now. If you make a mistake this time, that's O. K. If you are shy at first, don't worry. The next time it will be easier. The more mistakes you make and the more chances you take, the easier it will be to speak without fear.

What about grammar? What happens if you don't speak correct English? Of course, sometimes people might not always understand you, but even with speakers of our native language, we often need to explain things in a different way. If people don't understand what you say at first, you can try it again a different way. And if you don't understand another person, you can ask them again, and they will usually explain it another way until you understand.

> **"If you want to speak English, you must be willing to do two things: Make mistakes and take chances."**

Will this book help me?

Fast Fluency is filled with interesting communication activities that give you an opportunity to use your English to talk about all sorts of things. But you can't simply read it, you must speak with other people.

66Learning to speak a language can be a great adventure—if you are willing to be a little daring.99

If you study the conversations and variations in these lessons, practice speaking with your classmates, and discuss the topics given in this book, your English will definitely improve. You can learn to read a language alone in your room, with a dictionary and a grammar book, but you cannot learn to speak a language by yourself. You must have a conversation partner to talk with and something interesting to talk about.

Language and life are always full of surprises. When you are having a conversation with someone (in any language) you never know what the other person is going to say next. And like life itself, learning to speak a language can be a great adventure—if you are willing to be a little daring and take a few chances. It doesn't matter how good or bad your spoken English is now. If you study the material here and practice with your classmates, it will get better. That is a guarantee. Will your English be perfect? Of course not, but it will improve and you will have much more confidence *and* speaking ability when you finish this book. I hope you enjoy it. Good luck!

W. B.

To The Teacher

A CONVERSATIONAL TEXTBOOK should provide students with language they can use and it should furnish something they can talk about. This book strives to do both by offering the student concrete language and adult subject matter useful for communicating in contemporary, everyday English.

Most of us have never found the perfect textbook, and this one doubtless has its faults too, but I have tried to steer a course between the two extremes of conversational textbooks as I see them: an overabundance of content on the one hand and a concentration on structure to the detriment of communication and meaning on the other. While the assumption here is that students already have a basic working knowledge of English structure and lexicon, there is a consistent attempt to make students familiar with some of the most important functions and patterns of spoken English.

The premise of the book is that language is communication, not a puzzle, not a complex system of rules, not a medium for testing intelligence. The purpose of language is to communicate with other people on subjects of mutual interest to the speakers, whether that be finding out where the bus stops or discussing geopolitical issues. In this spirit, I have tried to give students ample material for practicing basic survival English as well as for expressing themselves on a wide variety of subjects.

There are twenty lessons, and teachers may cover them in any order. They are not graded, and each one contains very simple as well as more difficult and less frequently-used language items. While there is a certain logic to the presentation of the subject matter of the conversations, the level of difficulty remains more or less uniform throughout. Early lessons treat greetings, introductions, and small talk—topics and functions which often occur early in relationships or in initial encounters with strangers—but they need not be covered during the first few weeks of the course. It is not always easy for students to deal with these social functions early in the course when they are still uncomfortable talking with their classmates and may likely not even know them. These pedagogical matters are, of course, up to the individual teacher to

> **"Language is communication, not a puzzle, not a complex system of rules, not a medium for testing intelligence."**

decide. While the structural patterns and functional applications introduced throughout reflect the author's own preferences and experience, there was some effort to cover a repertoire of basic communication needs as suggested in standard inventories such as Van Ek and Alexander's *Threshold Level English* (Oxford: Pergamon Press, 1975).

Each lesson has a uniform format consisting of five parts:

Conversation

Variations

Your Turn

Sharing

Try Your Hand

> **"Each lesson has a uniform format consisting of five parts."**

Following is a brief summary of the format and character of each section with a few suggestions for teaching strategies.

Conversation

The "Conversation" sections which open each lesson seek to be as authentic as possible, with no artificial language. A major problem confronting the author of a conversational textbook is deciding which register to pitch the conversations at. While there are some examples of more formal English in many kinds of situations, including politeness language when talking to strangers, I have hoped to avoid the wooden quality that casts a pall of artificiality over so many textbooks which have the goal of teaching spoken English. Endeavoring to avoid cold and priggish textbook language that no native speakers in their right mind would ever utter, I have frequently included colloquial expressions such as "yeah," "uh, huh," "hmm," "let's see," and many other such pause markers and speech fillers. They remain opaque and lifeless on the page, of course, until the teacher models how they occur in an organic conversational and social context.

Also, though few textbooks ever take cognizance of it, English speakers quite frequently omit subject pronouns, particularly "I." Occasionally, I have tried to reflect this and other such elliptical tendencies in the conversations. If I have erred on the side of being too colloquial at times, I hope that teachers and students alike will find this transgression at least more desirable in the greater scheme of things than reinforcing the idea that spoken English is a robot-like language devoid of contractions, reduced forms, casual expressions, and—ultimately—bled dry of its lifeblood.

Variations

Immediately following the conversations in each lesson are six specific locutions drawn from the opening conversation along with examples of how they can change in everyday conversation. They are often picked up and practiced in subsequent exercises, frequently supplying much of the language used in the communicative exercises later in the lesson. By design, no directions accompany either the "Conversations" or the "Variations." Teachers are thereby at liberty to introduce and use the material in a variety of ways according to their own taste and style and the needs of individual classes.

Some teachers might be surprised to see what appear to be chimeric specters of the Audiolingual Method come back to haunt us in the form of pattern practices in disguise. The premises upon which this textbook are based differ drastically, of course, from orthodox ALM theory. Having been a student in French and German classes taught via the ALM in the fifties, and later teaching those languages myself through the ALM, I am definitely not espousing a return to the untinctured version of that approach. After teaching communicative ESL/EFL materials for several years, however, and observing students sometimes bewildered by a lack of specificity and definite language in many communicative textbooks, I saw a need for some concrete examples of the *shape* of English which can serve students as a conversational life preserver to embrace when they find themselves at sea conversationally. The pedagogical purpose of the "Variations", then, is to establish a sense of comfort with turns of phrase common in spoken English by giving students a feeling for the contours of the vernacular and helping them to develop an awareness of the kinds of variation possible.

While the patterns have the same format on the page (a combination of boldface and italic typefaces), there are actually two distinct types. Both employ an unchanging element (in boldface) with varied extensions (in italics). The difference lies in where the emphasis is. Frequently the main item of study is the unchanging boldface element. Such as the following (from Lesson 7):

> **Is there** *a department store* **around here?**
> *a bakery*
> *a supermarket*
> *a sporting goods store*
> *a library*

Less frequently, the main focus is on the italic element, and

> **"Teachers are at liberty to use the material in a variety of ways according to their own taste and style."**

synonymous expressions appear as variations, as in the following example (from Lesson 20):

How about you, **Pedro?**
> *what about you*
> *and you*
> *how do you feel about that*
> *what do you think*

Your Turn

The "Your Turn" section has an overtly communicative focus and is, in many respects, the heart of the textbook. Pair and group materials furnish a context for practicing the language or subject matter of each lesson, concentrating mainly on the functional language necessary for everyday survival (directions, requests, compliments, and the like).

In this section, students are asked to do a variety of activities designed to get them to talk to each other in English using whatever linguistic hooks and crooks they can come up with. They are not completely abandoned, however, for there are numerous suggestions for specific turns of phrase they can use, and language material gleaned from the "Conversations" and "Variations" portions of the lesson usually finds a natural fit here.

As teachers, we sometimes forget how intimidating pairwork can be for students who have but a little conversational facility. Many dyad and group activities appear deceptively simple and self-explanatory, but it is a risky pedagogical practice to supply a topic, picture, or activity, and then simply leave students to their own devices. In spite of its enshrinement as the reigning modality of communicative activities in the ESL classroom, pairwork is still not conventional communication. It *simulates* real communication, but it is not always a perfect match. As authentic as we might try to make communication activities in the classroom through developing materials and structuring the atmosphere of the location, inevitably a lingering artificiality remains. Therefore, exhaustive demonstration of how to do the pairwork activities is essential, and the involved teacher will monitor student's activities, coaching and supporting them with suggestions, hints, and encouragement.

> **"We some-times forget how intimidating pairwork can be for students who have but a little conversational facility."**

Sharing

The "Sharing" section introduces mature material for reflection and discussion. In keeping with the book's subtitle, *Communication in English for the International Age*, the themes introduced here have a global and cross-cultural flavor. There is also some attempt at sociolinguistic consciousness-raising, presented in the form of questions for small group work.

If the "Your Turn" section is the meat of the lesson, then surely the "Sharing" section must be the dessert. Here students are asked to move beyond the classroom and talk about real life, the world around them, and their own experience. Each section begins with a brief note pointing out some cultural aspect of English and English-speaking society or broader, international, socio-cultural topics. Then the students are asked to discuss with their classmates a variety of topics. The subject matter is usually related (if sometimes only loosely) to the material of the opening conversation. The scope of the topics is uniform for each lesson and expands on the subject matter, inviting students to share their own experience.

There are three general sets of topics for discussion which appear consistently in the following order in each lesson:

"Teacher intervention in modelling how to carry on a discussion is crucial."

I. Discussion topics which ask students to look at the customs of their own country. These opening reflections and discussions give students a grounding in their home culture which they can then use as a springboard to leap into a discussion of sociolinguistic and cultural contrasts in a more global context.

II. Topics which encourage the students to share details of their own past experience vis à vis the subject matter of the lesson. The emphasis here is on sharing personal impressions and feelings.

III. Topics which allow students to expand on their own experience by using their imagination or by seeing things in a broader, international context. This section sometimes suggests a certain fantasy situation or otherwise invites the student to engage in hypothetical thinking or to contemplate global issues.

While the material provided for conversational discussion here and elsewhere in the book is sometimes difficult, it strives always to be challenging and stimulating at an adult level. Once again, teacher intervention in modelling how to carry on a discussion is crucial here. One suggestion for structuring the discussion would be to divide the class into small groups and have each group select a discussion leader (rotating with each class meeting) and a scribe who takes notes and reports to the class later on the group's discussion. Without such structuring and frequent assistance by the teacher, students at this conversational level can quickly lose their focus.

Try Your Hand

The last section of each lesson has material for reading and vocabulary enrichment along with three short writing exercises. The material here ranges from letters, schedules, word lists, a menu, and a resumé to cultural matters, technology, and new terms in English.

Quite often, textbooks which emphasize oral communication ignore writing altogether. The primary goal of *Fast Fluency* is to improve skills in the spoken language, but since the students who will use this textbook probably have an imbalance of experience in writing and reading English, I have tried to capitalize on their existing strengths. The purpose of the writing exercises is to solidify conversational material already learned and give the students a feeling of confidence, security, and accomplishment.

The short writing assignments invite the students to use the reading material as a model, personalize it, and write something of their own. The topics here are often related to the material of the lessons and give students a further opportunity to apply the language they have just finished practicing. Teachers who do not wish to assign writing practice will find that the "Try Your Hand" sections easily adapt to oral discussion also, whether in pairs or small groups.

Illustrations

Illustrations occur throughout the book and are often related to the subject matter of the conversations and the practice material. While their spirit is often playful, teachers can nonetheless use the pictures and drawings as teaching aids. Simple questions to the students asking them to describe what they see can often get the conversational juices flowing. Some teachers may choose to use the illustrations as an impetus toward more communicative sharing by inviting the students to use their imaginations: "Who do you think is this?"; "What are these people doing?; "What are they thinking?; "Would you like to have dinner with this person?"; "Do you think you might enjoy taking a trip with her?"; "Would you like to ride on this bus?" Occasionally, a map or other visual material appears in connection with specific communication tasks. In such cases, there is an explanation of what students are supposed to do.

> **❝The purpose of the writing exercises is to solidify conversational material already learned and give the students a feeling of confidence, security, and accomplishment.❞**

Apologia

I have tried to put together a textbook which teaches students how to speak basic, colloquial English and which provides them with entertaining ways to practice and use their English. In addition to the conversational language we have come to expect, there is also material with a broader cultural perspective and an international focus.

I believe that if students are going to learn to speak English, they need something to talk about which engages their minds and personalities, not just patterns, pair work, and limited communication exercises. If you have nothing to talk about, conversation is impossible. Each lesson of this book takes the student from short conversations through pattern variations and pairwork on to an opportunity to exchange ideas and think about questions which affect the lives of everyone.

Facilitating communication across cultures and linguistic borders is the ultimate purpose of learning to speak any foreign language, but particularly is this true for English, which, as the international language, has an importance and utility far beyond the borders of English-speaking countries. Whether in an EFL or and ESL context, "conversation" is not simply the acquisition of survival level skills; students need and deserve more even in the earlier stages of their studies.

Whatever this book's shortcomings, and there surely are many, I hope that neither you nor your students will find it boring. I have tried to create a textbook that provides teachers a way to challenge students both linguistically and intellectually. You and your students will be the arbiters of the book's success in achieving these goals. I don't recall that Dante designated a special place in his *Inferno* reserved for the eternal torment of boring teachers, but there surely must be one down there somewhere in one of the lower *bolge*. I hope this book may in some small way serve to spare both you and me from that gruesome fate.

W. B.

"Facilitating communication across cultures is the ultimate purpose of learning any foreign language."

Fast Fluency

1   *Nice to meet you.*

Conversation

Mike: This is really a big reception, isn't it? [*party*]

Tom: There must be at least two hundred people here. [*min*]

Mike: Oh, look. There's Betty. Hello, Betty, how are things? [*you*]

Betty: Not too bad, Mike. I'd like you to meet my new roommate, Mayumi.

Mike: Hi, Mayumi, nice to meet you. This is my friend, Tom.

Tom: Nice meeting you, Mayumi.

Mayumi: Nice to meet you both.

Joanne: Mayumi's from Japan. She's going to be taking some English courses.

Mike: Oh, really. Say, isn't that Dr. Lee over there? He teaches in the Language Institute. Maybe you'd like to meet him.

Mayumi: Sure, why not? [*yes*]

Mike: Excuse me, Dr. Lee. I'd like to introduce you to a new student from Japan. This is Mayumi.

Dr. Lee: It's good to meet you, Mayumi.

Mayumi: Pleased to meet you, too, Dr. Lee. [*nice*]

Dr. Lee: Mayumi, let me introduce my wife, Ruth.

Mayumi: How do you do, Mrs. Lee?

Ms. Lee: I'm happy to meet you, Mayumi.

Nice to meet you.

Variations

Mike, *I'd like you to meet Mayumi.*
I'd like to introduce Joanne
this is Betty
let me introduce you to Dr. Lee
meet Tom

Hi, Mayumi, *nice to meet you.*
nice meeting you
it's good to meet you
pleased to meet you
I'm happy to meet you

She's going to be *taking some English courses.*
studying at the Language Institute
living in the dormitory — live and sleep
travelling to New York over Christmas (near)
staying for one semester

Say, isn't that *Dr. Lee* **over there?** Oh
the new English teacher
your roommate
the library
the school cafeteria

Maybe you'd like to *meet Dr. Lee.* my idea
have lunch tomorrow
go to the movies with me
tell me what's on your mind (think about)
study together tonight

Sure, *why not?*
I'd like to
I'd love to
that's fine with me
that sounds good to me

Your Turn

I. Go around to as many people as you can and introduce yourself. Choose some of the following language. Don't forget to shake hands and look the person in the eye.

Hi, I'm _____.
Hello, my name is _____.
How are you? I'm _____.
But you can call me _____.
Just call me _____.
I'm from _____.
I'm majoring in _____.
I live in _____.

II. Ask if your partner would like to meet another classmate. (Make sure you know the other person's name first.) Then introduce the two of them.

Maybe you'd like to meet _____.
Would you like to meet _____?
Let me introduce _____.
I'd like you to meet _____.
This is _____.

III. Introduce your partner to a few other people. Then let him introduce you to some other classmates. Use the appropriate language for meeting people. Ask how to spell the other person's name. Then find out which name is their first name (given name) or last name (family name). Choose some of the following questions.

How do you spell that?
What's your first name?
What's your last name?
Is that your first name or last name?
Is your name French (German, Arabic, Spanish, Japanese, Chinese, etc.)?

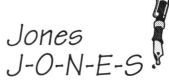

IV. Write down the names of five or six famous people. Don't show them to your partner. Then say the names and ask for the spelling.

A: Have you ever heard of _____?
B: Of course./Sure.
A: Can you spell her/his name?

Sharing

Meeting new people is an important social activity. In addition to using some of the phrases you have practiced in this lesson, shaking hands and looking the person you are meeting in the eye (eye contact) are often essential non-verbal skills you need when you meet someone in English. The word "nice" is very common in introductions and greetings and is, in fact, one of the most common words in spoken English. Notice the many different contexts where it is used throughout this book.

I. Every culture has special social rituals for meeting people. What are some of the things you say and do in your country when meeting someone for the first time? Are there any differences from introductions in English? Any similarities?

II. In your own experience, have you ever met a person who was important, unusual, interesting, or inspiring? Talk about what it was like. What did you say? What did the other person say?

III. Have you ever wanted to meet a famous person? Who are the three people in the world you would most like to meet? Why? Share with your classmates what you would say to these people if you had a chance to meet them and chat with them.

Try Your Hand

Read the following letter and then write on the topics below.

CENTRAL COLLEGE

Hi!

    I'm Jack Taylor, and I just found out you are going to be my roommate next year. Let me tell you a little about myself. I am majoring in Economics, and my favorite course is macroeconomics. I like jazz music a lot, and my favorite singer is Ella Fitzgerald.

    After I graduate, I hope to work in international banking and to live in Europe and Asia. I am quite interested in other countries and enjoy meeting people from abroad. Of course, I also like to travel.

    I'm really looking forward to meeting you. Please write if you have time.

        Sincerely,

        Jack

Topic One
Write a short note to Jack Taylor introducing yourself.

Topic Two
Describe Jack Taylor in a note to a friend.

Topic Three
Write a brief description of your best friend.

Do you live near here?

Conversation

Dr. Lee: There are so many new faces at this reception.

Ms. Lee: I can hardly believe it.

Do you live near here, Mayumi?

Mayumi: Yes, I live on campus in a dorm. *(the land of college)*

Dr. Lee: How do you like campus life?

Mayumi: To tell you the truth, things

were a little difficult at first,

but now I'm getting used to being here.

Ms. Lee: Where are you from in Japan?

Mayumi: I'm from Kyoto.

Ms. Lee: That's supposed to be a beautiful city.

Mayumi: Well, there are lots of famous places there.

Dr. Lee: By the way, what's your major, Mayumi?

Mayumi: International Relations.

Dr. Lee: Oh, is that right! *(is interesting)*

Ms. Lee: How interesting!

I guess you like it.

Mayumi: Well, it keeps me busy.

Ms. Lee: I'll bet it does. *sure, I think*

Variations

I can hardly *believe it.*
     wait till spring vacation
     remember everybody's name
     afford a new car
     understand this chapter

How do you like *campus life?*
     living in America
     your history teacher
     working at MacDonald's
     this party

To tell you the truth, *things were difficult.*
     I didn't understand much when I arrived
     my neighbors are a little noisy
     I'd rather live off-campus
     I failed the chemistry exam

That's supposed to be *a beautiful city.*
     an interesting field
     the best newspaper in America
     one of the oldest buildings in Europe
     a difficult language to learn

By the way, *what's your major?*
     who's your roommate
     that's Dr. Lee over there
     how do you like your new job
     let's have lunch together soon

Oh, *is that right!*
     how interesting
     really
     you don't say
     that's fascinating

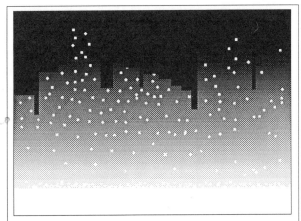

Your Turn

I. Find out as much as you can about your partner. Take some notes and be prepared to tell someone else or a group what you have found out.

Here are some things to ask about:

name/nicknames
hometown (born)
family
current living situation (now)
job
favorite subject (study)
major field — " —
favorite activities (like to do)
hobbies
likes/dislikes
travel

> Do you like PETS?

Use some of the following language:

Do you like _____?
How do you like _____?
What do you like about _____?
Where do you live?
What do you like to do on weekends?
How do you spend your free time?
What's your favorite _____?
Who's your favorite _____?

II. Now talk about your partner to someone else (another student, a small group, or the whole class). Tell them all the important information you learned in activity "I" above.

III. Tell the class about your country and your hometown or the region where you are from. Where is it? What are the main attractions? Is it famous for anything in particular? What do you like or dislike about it? What was it like growing up there? What is the most interesting building? Who is the most interesting person from there?

Sharing

When we start a conversation in English, whether with friends or strangers, there is usually a short warm-up period. If we don't know the person, we usually ask questions about where they are from or how they like something. Depending on the situation, we can talk about work or family also. This is called "small talk." Such harmless and trivial exchange is important for establishing a conversational relationship. Even with friends, we often talk about the weather or other general topics before going on to more important matters. With strangers, the kinds of opening questions vary with the culture.

I. Is there "small talk" in your native language? What kinds of things do you talk about with someone you have just met? Does the content depend on the nationality, age, or social status of the other person? Are there any taboo subjects? What do you talk about with friends after the initial greeting? How and when did you learn these customs?

II. Have you ever had any surprising or unusual conversations with strangers in your native language? What did you talk about? What did the other person do or say that was strange?

III. Have you ever seen a movie or television program in English? Did the characters use small talk? How was it like or unlike greetings and small talk in your native language? Do you think it is O. K. to speak English using the rules of your own culture about the subject matter of small talk? Can you see any dangers in this?

Try Your Hand

Read the following list of nicknames and then write on the topics below.

NICKNAMES

Men		Women	
Albert	Al	Catherine	Cathy
Andrew	Andy	Christine	Chris
Anthony	Tony	Deborah	Debbie
Charles	Charlie	Eleanor	Ella
David	Dave	Elizabeth	Betty
Douglas	Doug	Jaqueline	Jackie
Edward	Ed	Jennifer	Jenny
Francis	Frank	Judith	Judy
John	Jack	Julia	Julie
Joseph	Joe	Margaret	Meg
Lawrence	Larry	Marjory	Marge
Michael	Mike	Martha	Marty
Peter	Pete	Patricia	Patty
Richard	Dick	Rebecca	Becky
Robert	Bob	Sandra	Sandy
Stephen	Steve	Suzanne	Sue
Thomas	Tom	Virginia	Ginny

Topic One

Write about some typical nicknames in English.

Topic Two

Make a list of names and nicknames in your native language.

Topic Three

Explain to someone from another country how your native language uses nicknames.

Hi, how are you doing?

Conversation

Tom: Hi, Joanne, how are you doing?

Joanne: Not bad, Tom, how about you?

Tom: Oh, I'm O. K.

Joanne: Just O. K.? I heard you and Mike found a great new apartment.

Tom: Yeah, it's pretty nice, but the problem is we have to move, and that's no fun.

Joanne: I agree. Well, look who's here.

Mike: Hello there, Joanne, how are things going?

Joanne: Pretty good, Mike. How have you been doing?

Mike: Well, staying fairly busy.

Tom: Did you talk to the landlord yet?

Mike: Yeah, we can move in on the thirtieth. One day early.

Tom: Wonderful! I can't wait.

Mike: Me either.

Joanne: Listen, you guys, I have to be going now. It was good seeing you.

Tom: Nice to see you, too, Joanne.

Mike: Take care.

Joanne: Bye now.

Mike: See you later.

Variations

Hi, *how are you doing?*
how are things going
how have you been
how have things been
how have you been doing

Oh, I'm *O. K.*
alright
not bad
so so
pretty good

Wonderful! **I can't wait.**
terrific
great
marvelous
fantastic

Listen, *I have to be going now.*
I must be going now
I have to run (*it's time to leave*)
I need to go now
I have to get going

Nice to see you, **Joanne.**
good seeing you
nice talking to you
enjoyed seeing you
good to see you again

Bye now, *take care.*
see you later
so long
have a nice day
take it easy

good buy

Your Turn

I. Say "hi" to your partner and to as many other people as you can. Be sure to use first names. If they are far away from you, wave to them when you say hello. Use as many variations as you can when greeting people and when answering them.

II. Say hello to your partner and ask about her or his neighborhood, apartment, house, roommates, family, pets, and the like. Switch roles and talk about your living situation. Finally, say you have to be going and then leave.

III. Now have several short conversations with different people like this:

Say hello to several different classmates.

Tell each of them something about yourself, something that happened recently, or something you are going to do.

Tell them you have to leave and say goodbye.

Here are some subjects you can talk about:

your parents, friends, spouse, etc.
what you did last weekend
your dog
new clothes
a CD
your favorite pianist
a club you belong to
good food
the recent news
a TV program
your job
a movie
a problem
some good news
some bad news
your social life (or lack of it)
a concert

Sharing

Where we live, pray, and play is important to all of us. Various cultures view space differently, but people in many countries separate homes, churches, and places of entertainment. In public places, we know who stands where in a line or who sits in a certain place in the dining room or church. In other cultures, the rules are sometimes different. Breaking the rules or violating space taboos can be as dangerous as serious errors in language communication. We must know both to communicate well.

I. How is space divided up in your culture? Where do people live, pray, and play? Are they separate? How can you tell these places apart? Are there any special rules or taboos about space and places?

can not do

II. Have you ever gone into a place where you were not supposed to go? What happened? Why did you go there?

III. In some countries, there are strict rules about where people can go. At one time in certain parts of the United States, black people were not allowed to ride in the front of public buses or to use toilet facilities with white people. South African *apartheid* laws also have closed certain spaces to black people. In some countries women are forbidden to enter certain places. Have you heard of any other such customs or laws in the world? How do you feel about them?

Try Your Hand

The floor plan below is related to Topic One. The other topics deal with real and imaginary places.

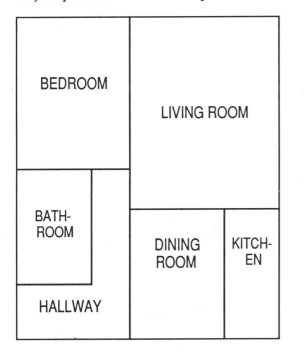

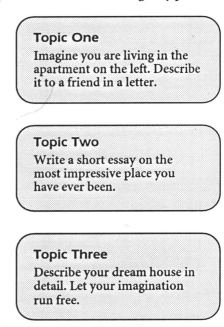

Topic One
Imagine you are living in the apartment on the left. Describe it to a friend in a letter.

Topic Two
Write a short essay on the most impressive place you have ever been.

Topic Three
Describe your dream house in detail. Let your imagination run free.

4 *Hello, this is Mike calling.*

Conversation

Ring . . . Riinng . . . Riiinnng

Voice: Hello.   *could, can (to)*

Mike: Hello, may I speak with Mayumi?

Voice: *wait* Hold on a second, please.

Mayumi: Hello, this is Mayumi.

Mike: Hello, Mayumi, this is Mike calling.   *speaking*

Mayumi: Oh hi, Mike.

Mike: Listen, Mayumi, I was wondering if you would *(am) hope (would you like)*

         like to go to the movies with me next Saturday.

Mayumi: I'd love to. Did you have any particular movie in mind? *specific* *to think*

Mike: Well, how about that new Woody Allen movie? *my idea*

Mayumi: That sounds great. Where should we meet? *like*

Mike: Hmm, let's see, we could meet at the Cedar Hills Shopping Center. *thinking*

Mayumi: Sounds good. What time should I be there?

Mike: The first showing is at 2:00, so why *let us, my idea*

         don't we meet about 1:00 and have a

         fast lunch quick sandwich before the movie?

Mayumi: That sounds O. K. to me.

Mike: Well, it was nice talking

         to you, Mayumi.

Mayumi: I'll see you Saturday,

         Mike. Bye now.

Mike: Bye .

Variations

Hello, *may I speak with Mayumi?*
       is Mike in
       could I speak with Pedro
       I'd like to speak with Mr. Brown, please
       could you give me the sales department

hope, think

I was wondering if *you would like to go to the movies.* *(one)*
       you have time for a chat *(talk)* *(in the future)* */sometimes)*
       you'd like to play tennis sometime *woega*
       you'd like to have dinner together soon
       you'd like to join us for bridge on Sunday

my idea

How about *that new Woody Allen movie?*
       going to the Madonna concert
       a quick sandwich
       calling me tomorrow
       meeting at 1:00

That sounds *great.*
       good
       wonderful
       like fun
       terrific

Let's do

Why don't we *meet about 1:00?*
       go to the baseball game together
       try that new pizza place
       talk tomorrow on the phone
       have a drink together soon

(also)

Well, *it was nice talking to you.*
       I enjoyed talking with you
       it was good chatting with you
       it was nice to hear from you
       thanks for calling

Your Turn

I. With your partner, practice using telephone language. Since you can't see people on the other end of the telephone line, look away from your partner when you talk so that you can't give or receive non-verbal hints. Call and invite your partner to do some of the following. Then change roles, and your partner will call you.

go out for coffee
study together for the test
go to Disneyland
have a pizza
play football
see "Back to the Future"
visit the Metropolitan Museum
go camping
go out dancing

II. You need to make an appointment at the places listed at the bottom of the page. Take turns playing the telephone receptionist. Here is some telephone language you can use:

A: I'd like to make an appointment with _____ for next Tuesday.
yes – *B: Certainly. What time?*
A: Three o'clock.   expect to come
B: Three o'clock is fine. We'll look for you then.

A: Could I possibly see _____ on the thirtieth at _____ o'clock?
B: I'm sorry, we're all booked up then.
A: How about on <u>Oct</u> *at* <u>3</u> ?
B. Yes. That's open. See you then.

(booked out) (ok)

Alan Kee, M.D. medical General Medicine	Dival Nasone Hairstyling for Ladies & Gentlemen	George Arai Attorney at Law *We take care of all your legal needs.*	Wu Lee Acupuncture Clinic ⋆⋆⋆ Holistic – all body. Health Care
✿ **Family Counselling Center** *Private and Group Therapy By Appointment Only.*	OUT WEST TAILORS WESTERN ATTIRE CALL FOR A FITTING	A.R. Black Income Tax Consultants By Appointment	*Bonnard Studios* Photography with Flair

Sharing

Language is only one aspect of communication. Non-verbal gestures and signals are sometimes even more important than words. A nod of the head, a wave of the hand can often express more meaning than dozens of words. Non-verbal communication varies with the culture, and using the wrong gestures can be disastrous. We miss non-verbal communication when talking on the telephone in a foreign language. Suddenly, the non-verbal hints are not there, and we must depend on sounds alone to understand our conversation partner.

I. Can you think of some non-verbal signals or gestures common in your country? What do people do when they say hello or good-bye, when they apologize, when they are sad, happy, embarrassed, surprised?

II. Gesture and movement are important in dramatic presentations. Have you ever seen a movie or a play where you noticed this? Have you ever been to the ballet or to other kinds of dance performances which tell a story? What was it like?

III. Since English is the international language, many people study it, but what about the non-verbal aspect of communication? What happens if we speak English but use non-verbal signals from another culture? When communicating internationally in English, how can we solve the differences in non-verbal communication between countries and cultures?

Try Your Hand

Study the following list and then write on the topics below.

Famous Inventions

Date	Invention	Inventor
1447	Movable Type	Gutenberg (Germany)
1583	Pendulum	Galileo (Italy)
1608	Telescope	Lippershey (Netherlands)
1642	Adding Machine	Pascal (France)
1709	Piano	Cristofori (Italy)
1829	Locomotive	Stephenson (England)
1835	Photography	Daguerre (France)
1876	Telephone	Bell (U. S. A.)
1877	Phonograph	Edison (U. S. A.)
1889	Automobile	Daimler (Germany)
1895	Radio	Marconi (Italy)
1903	Airplane	Wright Bros. (U. S. A.)

Topic One

Choose one of the inventions and write about its importance in your life.

Topic Two

Write a short note about any inventor on the list.

Topic Three

What invention do you think has changed the world more than any other? Explain why.

5 *Do you happen to know . . . ?*

Conversation

Mayumi: Excuse me, but I need to get to the Cedar Hills Shopping Center.
Do you happen to know which bus I should take?

Lady: Uh, let me see. I'm pretty sure it's number 44.

Mayumi: I see. And could you tell me where the bus stop is?

Lady: Oh, sure. It's right over there, across the street.

Mayumi: Thanks so much. Do you by any chance know how long it takes to get

there from here?

Lady: Oh, I'd say about twenty minutes or so.

Mayumi: Do you mind if I ask you one last question?

Lady: Sure, no problem.

Mayumi: Do you happen to know how much the bus fare is?

Lady: I'm fairly sure it's sixty cents, but you'd better ask the driver just to be
on the safe side.

Mayumi: O. K. Thanks a lot. I really appreciate your help.

Lady: Not at all. Glad to be of help. You'd better hurry, though, the bus is

coming now. Good luck finding the Shopping Center.

Mayumi: Thanks a million.

Lady: You bet.

Variations

I need to *get to the shopping center.*
    catch the bus
    take a break
    do some shopping
    meet my friend, Tom

[handwritten: not shure]

Do you happen to *know which bus I should take?*
    have a map of the city
    have some time this afternoon
    know what time the show starts
    have a spare pen   *[handwritten: one more (my sure)]*

Could you tell me *where the bus stop is?*
    when the next flight leaves
    how to get downtown
    who is in charge of sales   *[handwritten: (the boss) responsible]*
    how much this costs

[handwritten: not shure]

Do you by any chance *know how long it takes?*
    need a new car
    remember her name
    have the time
    watch the evening news

Thanks *a lot.*
    so much
    very much
    a million
[handwritten: a lot =]   <u>*loads*</u> *[handwritten: very much]*

> IT'S RIGHT OVER THERE.

Not at all. **Glad to be of help.**
    don't mention it *[handwritten: (don't talk about)]*
    you bet
    no problem
    no trouble at all

Your Turn

I. Below are some symbols you often see in public places. Take turns asking your partner what they mean. Here is some suggested language:

Do you by any chance know . . . ?   *Could you tell me . . . ?*
Do you happen to know . . . ?   *Do you mind if I ask you . . . ?*

alcohol.

II. Almost everyone knows how to DO at least one thing well. It may be our job, our major in school, our hobby, a sport, playing a musical instrument, or something else. Find out what your partner knows how to make or do best. Then ask her or him to tell you as much as possible about that activity. Ask as many questions about that subject as you can. Be specific. Then tell your partner what you can do best and answer his or her questions about it.

III. Partner A is Chief of Detectives at the International Bureau of Investgation (IBI). Partner B is an investigator and must find out all the information about a new case and what the IBI's mission is. Here are the cases below. Partner A explains case 1; then Partner B explains case 2. DON'T LOOK AT YOUR PARTNER'S CASE DESCRIPTION. What was stolen? How much is it worth? Who stole it? Why? Where? When? For what purpose? How serious is the case? What can we do?

CASE 1 (Partner A): A priceless pearl necklace, "the Mermaid's Tears," has been stolen. Its value is over a million dollars. It belongs to the Queen of the ancient Mediterranean country of Luxadora. The King doesn't want the press to know about the theft. The IBI's mission is to recover the necklace quietly and quickly. The only clue is a note signed with "V".

CASE 2 (Partner B): Poison was stolen from a laboratory in the capital city of Zeronagrad. There is enough poison to kill the entire city. Terrorists have made a phone call to the mayor and want all political prisoners freed or they will pour the poison in the water supply. The IBI's mission is to find out who stole the poison, get the poison back, and to capture the terrorists dead or alive.

Sharing

Communication is no longer simply a face-to-face activity. The mails, the telephone, and the telegraph have been with us for years, and now facsimile transmission (FAX), copiers, digital storage, computers, and satellites enable us to find out what we need to know almost instantly. English is by far the most frequently-used language when messages are sent around the world through these new media. In this sense, English has come to play a central role in the "information revolution" and the "communication revolution."

I. In the United States, one third of all people use a computer regularly. Are computers widely used in your country? Who uses them? What for? Do you feel that computers are an important aspect of life in your country? What about satellites? How about cable television?

II. How do you get the information you need? Through books? Radio? Television? Other media? When you write, do you simply use a pen or pencil? Do you know how to type? Have you ever used a computer? What for? Do you watch television very much? Do you watch video movies at home? How do you feel about the new communications media?

III. Do you think the new communications media mentioned above are changing the world for the better? If so, discuss some of the positive aspects of modern communications technology. If not, what is the negative side of these inventions?

Try Your Hand

Look at the following definitions and then write on the topics below.

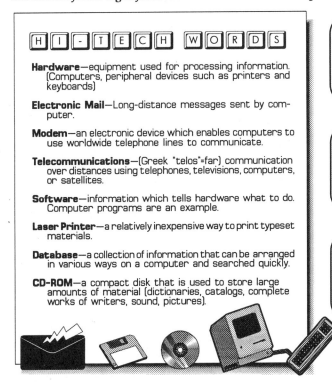

H I - T E C H   W O R D S

Hardware—equipment used for processing information. (Computers, peripheral devices such as printers and keyboards)

Electronic Mail—Long-distance messages sent by computer.

Modem—an electronic device which enables computers to use worldwide telephone lines to communicate.

Telecommunications—(Greek "telos"=far) communication over distances using telephones, televisions, computers, or satellites.

Software—information which tells hardware what to do. Computer programs are an example.

Laser Printer—a relatively inexpensive way to print typeset materials.

Database—a collection of information that can be arranged in various ways on a computer and searched quickly.

CD-ROM—a compact disk that is used to store large amounts of material (dictionaries, catalogs, complete works of writers, sound, pictures).

Topic One
What effect has technology had on your everyday life? Write a short essay of explanation.

Topic Two
Write a short note asking an expert to explain three things you don't understand about computers.

Topic Three
Some people say computers are dangerous. Write a short essay explaining why you agree or disagree.

6 *Go straight down this street.*

on
(south)
up (north)

Conversation

Mayumi: Pardon me, but I'm looking for the Cedar Hills Shopping Center. Could you please tell me how to get there?

Man: Well, let me think now. You go straight down this street and take a left at the next corner.

go
turn

Mayumi: Uh, huh. *(a TA)*

Man: Then you'll see a large supermarket on the right. O. K.?

Mayumi: O. K.

Man: Go past that supermarket and turn right at the next traffic signal. You'll find the shopping center on the left hand side of the street, in the middle of the block, across from the bank.

lights
traffic signal

Mayumi: I see. Left at the next corner and then right at the stoplight.

Man: Exactly. You've got it.

correct have got

Mayumi: That sounds pretty easy.

directions

Thanks so much.

Man: Just be careful not to take the wrong turn at the stoplight.

makes drive

Mayumi: I will.

Thanks so much.

Man: My pleasure. Don't mention it.

you are welcome

NORTH POLE

Variations

Pardon me, but I'm looking for *the shopping center.* *(help me)*

> *a bookstore*
> *the nearest gas station*
> *the rest room* *(toilet)* *bathroom washroom, lavatory. (public.)*
> *the closest post office*

Well, *let me think now.* *(before answer) thinking. (us)*

> *let's see now*
> *just a second*
> *let me think a minute*
> *let me see now*

Go straight down this street and *take a left.*

> *turn right* *= turn*
> *go left* *= "*
> *bear right* *= (turn) – (po guns) (turn)*
> *hang a left* *(~ ~)*
> *take = make*

Exactly. *You've got it.* *(under stand)*

> *you understand*
> *that's it* *(correct)*
> *you're right*
> *you'll have no problem*

That sounds *pretty easy.* *} close to*

> *fairly simple } *
> *difficult*
> *hard to find*
> *easy to get to* *(to go that)*

Just be careful *not to take the wrong turn.* *(make)*

> *to go straight down this street*
> *you don't make the wrong turn*
> *of the traffic*
> *about arriving on time*

Your Turn

I. Here are two different versions of the same map, one for Partner A, one for Partner B. Choose one map and cover the other one. DO NOT LOOK AT YOUR PARTNER'S MAP. Find out the missing information from your partner. You are both at the corner of Washington and Broad.

PARTNER A:

Ask your partner where the following places are and write the answers on your map.

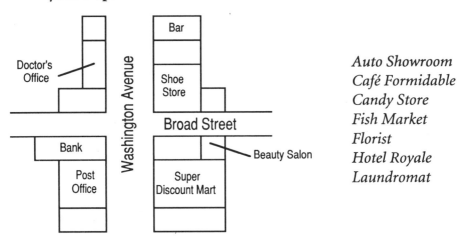

Auto Showroom
Café Formidable
Candy Store
Fish Market
Florist
Hotel Royale
Laundromat

PARTNER B:

Ask your partner where the following places are and write the answers on your map.

Bank
Bar
Beauty Salon
Doctor's Office
Post Office
Shoe Store
Super Discount Mart

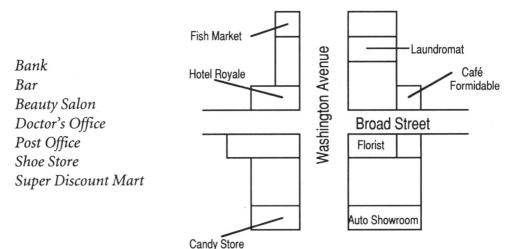

II. Your partner is coming to visit. Draw a map of where you live. Then explain how to get to your house. Make sure your partner understands. Switch roles.

Sharing

As the world gets smaller, distant countries do not seem so far away. Modern air travel has brought us closer together in the Global Village, yet we still live in a place we call home. Most of us feel a sense of loyalty to our native country and love our native language. English is the international language because of various historical and political accidents. Although its spelling is especially difficult (even for native speakers), it is no better or worse than any other language. If we can speak, read, and understand English, however, our opportunities to communicate internationally are much greater.

I. In India, the Philippines, and some other countries, English is widely used among the residents. Is this the case in your country? If so, why? If not, do many people study English? Why? Which English words have come into your native language?

II. Why are you studying English? What do you like about it? What do you dislike about it? Have you ever spoken English with someone from another country? Could you understand them? What did you talk about? Can you always understand your English teacher? What do you find most difficult about this class? The most enjoyable?

III. What do you think about the idea of English as an international language? Is it a dangerous situation? Do you think Anglo-Saxon culture and values are being spread through English study? Do you associate English with Christianity? If you could make another language the international language, which one would you choose? Why?

Try Your Hand

Using the following map for reference, write on the topics below.

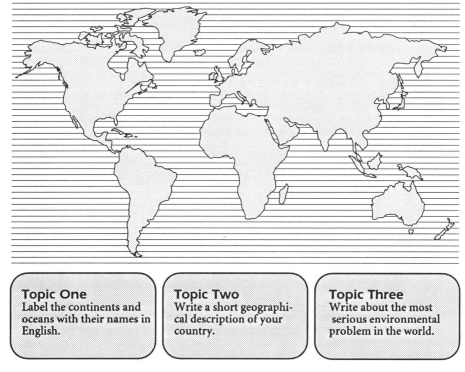

Topic One
Label the continents and oceans with their names in English.

Topic Two
Write a short geographical description of your country.

Topic Three
Write about the most serious environmental problem in the world.

7 *May I help you?*

Conversation

Mike: Did you have any trouble finding the shopping center?

Mayumi: Not at all. Several people helped me with the directions, and it wasn't

so hard. Say, Mike, it's getting cool and I need to buy a sweater. Is there

a department store around here?

Mike: Oh sure, there're several. How about that one over there?

(They enter the department store.)

Salesclerk: May I help you?

Mayumi: Do you carry pullover sweaters in my size?

Salesclerk: Yes, I'm sure we do. What color were you interested in?

Mayumi: Do you have something in grey or navy?

Salesclerk: Certainly. Why don't you try this one on for size?

Mayumi: It fits perfectly. How do you like it, Mike?

Mike: Well, uh, it looks fine to me.

Mayumi: I'll take it.

Salesclerk: Yes, ma'am. Please pay the cashier.

Right over there.

Mike: Mayumi, we'd better hurry up.

The movie is starting in

about fifteen minutes.

Mayumi: Oh, gosh, I'm sorry.

I didn't realize it was getting so late.

Variations

Did you have any trouble finding *the shopping center?*
    the bus stop
    the bank
    the post office
    the bookstore

It wasn't so *hard.*
    difficult
    interesting
    amusing = enjoy = interest   amazing — terrific, fantastic, surprise, marvelous, wonderful.
    long

Is there *a department store* **around here?**
    a bakery
    a supermarket
    a sporting goods store
    a library

Oh sure, there're *several.*   a few
    lots
    plenty   many = lot.
    two or three
    more than enough = more) we need.

Do you have something in *navy?*   carry
    a light color
    a dark color
    leather
    my size

We'd better *hurry up.*   = get going   / should.
    get going
    have lunch
    call home
    study for the test

Your Turn

I. Ask your partner about the following topics.
Use: *You didn't . . . did you?*

have trouble finding the shop
find my gloves
get caught in traffic
fail the exam
apply for that job
buy a new computer
lose your wallet
feed the parrot
wreck your car

II. You are the shopper and your partner is the salesclerk in a department store.
Use questions and answers like these and ask for the items below:

Do you have _____? Yes, I'm sure we do. This way, please.
Do you carry _____? I believe so. Try the third floor.

VCR's
ladies' hosiery
men's dress shirts
hair care products
men's toiletries
kitchen utensils
china
perfume
underwear
ties
crystal

III. You need to find out if there is somewhere near here that carries the following items. Be sure to use the correct name of the place that sells the things you want to buy.

tires	*tee shirts*
gasoline	*baseball gloves*
swimming trunks	*vegetables*
paintings	*television sets*
computer games	*hats*
pens and pencils	*stamps*

Sharing

not hessesary *top robust 26 a*

Shopping is a universal activity. We buy things, ranging from food and drink for survival to luxury items like cars and yachts. Every culture has a different style for shopping. In the Middle East, it is popular to bargain with the shopkeepers about the price. They expect it. In other countries, it would be considered rude and improper. In English there are certain politeness formulas that are standard in shopping situations. "May I help you?" or "Can I get something for you?" are two of these.

impolite *not correct*

I. How do people shop in your country? Is bargaining or "haggling" about prices expected? What kind of special sales or discounts are there where you live? Are most of the food stores small "mom and pop" operations or are they large supermarkets?

II. Do you like to shop? What do you like to buy? How often do you go shopping? Are you a "smart" shopper? Do you compare prices before you buy? If you have had any unusual experiences while shopping, share them with your classmates.

III. Have you ever ordered anything by mail? What was it? How did you go about ordering it and how was it delivered? What do you think about credit cards, or "plastic money," as they are sometimes called? Are credit cards convenient? Perhaps, too convenient? Do you think it is wise to buy on credit? Are there any dangers?

Try Your Hand

Read the following page from a mail order catalog and then write on the topics below.

R. R. Brean, Ltd.
Since 1887
"Everything for the Outdoors"

Cotton Turtleneck Shirt	$16.00
Basic for Cool Weather	
Suede Jacket	$265.00
Style with Warmth	
All Wool Sweaters	$47.50
100% Lamb	
Corduroy Trousers	$35.00
Rugged and Stylish	
Mounaineer Socks	$10.00
Double Lining	
Hiking Boots	$95.00
Hard as Nails	
Day Pack	$27.00
Big and Sturdy	
Leather Gloves	$30.00
Water Resistant	

Topic One
Order by mail some of the items from R. R. Brean's Catalog.

Topic Two
Write a letter asking for more information about some of the items on the left.

Topic Three
You made a mistake ordering. Explain this to R. R. Brean and ask for an exchange.

That's a nice sweater.

Conversation

Joanne: That's a nice sweater you're wearing, Mayumi.

Mayumi: Thanks, Joanne. I just got it recently, and it was a real bargain.

Joanne: I need to buy some new clothes myself.

Mayumi: Why, Joanne, I think you're such a good dresser.

Joanne: That's nice of you to say so, Mayumi,

but I'm sort of tired of my clothes.

Mayumi: Well, why don't we go shopping together sometime?

Joanne: O. K. That's a deal. But for the next few days

I'm going to be studying for exams.

Mayumi: Me, too. I used to have a lot more free time,

but this year I'm busier than ever.

Joanne: When I was in high school,

I used to go out every weekend,

but now I spend most of

my time studying.

Mayumi: I know what you mean.

Joanne: Anyway, after next week,

I'll have some free time

and we can get together then.

Mayumi: I'm looking forward to it.

Variations

That's *nice* of you to say so.
    kind ~ отзывчивый, добрый
    sweet
    good
    generous ~ щедрый и великодушный

слегка
I'm sort of *tired*. надоел
    bored наскучил
    busy
    eager нетерпеливый
    curious любопытный

Why don't we *go shopping* together sometime? как-нибудь?
    have lunch
    try that new restaurant
    have coffee
    take a trip

For the next few days I'm going to be *studying*.
    working
    visiting my parents
    staying at home
    typing my paper

When I was in high school, I used to *go out every weekend*.
    have a lot more free time
    go dancing once a week
    enjoy myself more
    date more often

I spend most of my time *studying*.
    reading books
    talking on the phone
    writing letters
    playing basketball

Your Turn

I. **Practice giving compliments to each other.**
Partner A gives B a compliment using:
"That's a nice . . . ."
"I like your . . . ."
B replies: *"Thanks, that's nice of you to say so."*

THAT'S NICE OF YOU TO SAY SO.

I LIKE YOUR HAIRDO.

Suggestions for compliments:
new haircut
watch
shirt
car
parents
tennis serve (wagara) (tyle)
sense of humor (laugh)
friends
new gloves
cap

II. **Tell your partner what your plans for the immediate future are.** Use the following language:

I'm going to be studying.
I'm going to be leaving for Brussels.

III. **Now choose a friend or a family member and tell your partner what that person is going to be doing soon.**

When I was a baby, I was cute.

I used to be a good boy.

IV. **Talk about what you used to do in the past and how things used to be.** Here are some time expressions you can use:

when I was in junior high
several years ago
back then
a long time ago
during my high school days

Sharing

Compliments are positive comments we make to people, saying that we like something about their appearance, talents, skills, or something they own. Compliments often make us feel good, but sometimes they can embarrass us or make us feel insecure. The kinds of compliments permitted differ according to the culture we live in. Also, there are definite, yet unspoken, rules about the way we should accept compliments. In English, we usually thank the person who gives the compliment and then explain why the quality or item complimented is not really so valuable or important.

I. Are compliments frequent in your native language? What do people give compliments about in your country? Is there special language for compliments? What should you say when someone gives you a compliment in your native language?

II. Do you enjoy receiving compliments? Have you ever felt someone was giving you a compliment because they wanted something from you? Do you give other people compliments very often? How do you feel when you do?

III. What is the difference between compliments and flattery? In some cultures there is little or no distinction between the two. When you are communicating with people from other countries in English, how should you give and receive compliments? It is impossible to know all of the social rules for every culture in the world. As international citizens, what should we do?

Try Your Hand

Read the following letter and then write on the topics below.

DIGITECHNO, LTD.
Tokyo, Japan

Mr. Douglas Schwarz
Department of Energy
Washington, DC

Dear Mr. Schwarz:

Thank you so much for your kind attention last week when my colleagues and I were in Washington. Our discussions with you were extremely informative. You have an excellent staff.

It was very thoughtful of you to take us to Kennedy Center for the concert by the National Symphony. We also enjoyed the tour of the Library of Congress and the Museum of Science and Technology.

You and your staff were helpful in many ways, and I would like to express our appreciation. The next time you are in Japan, I hope you will let us know.

Sincerely yours,

Hiroko Watanabe

Hiroko Watanabe

Topic One
Answer Ms. Watanabe's letter. Tell her you will be in Tokyo next month.

Topic Two
Write a note thanking a business colleague for hospitality.

Topic Three
Drop a thank-you note to your boss's wife for her recent party.

I'm trying to study.

Conversation

Tom: What are you doing, Mike?

Mike: I'm trying to study, but I'm not having much luck. *(not success)*

Tom: You've been working too much lately, don't you think? *recently*

Why don't you take a break?

Mike: I'm reading the last chapter now,

and then I'm thinking about going to the gym. *(gymnasium)*

Tom: Good for you! I've been meaning to study, *idea* *I think (fact)*

but I can't get my mind on school lately. By the way, *hard for me thinking* *(change the subject)*

did you invite Mayumi to our party yet?

Mike: I've been trying to call her for the past few days,

but the line is always busy.

Tom: She's no doubt talking to Joanne. *sure (positive – 100%)*

I think they're planning a program for the

International Relations Club for next week.

Mike: Well, I'm leaving for

Beginning the gym now. See you later.

Tom: O. K. Have a nice time.

Variations

You've been *working too much.*
    sleeping too late (wake up late/in the morning)
    watching television a lot
    losing weight fast
    staying home too much

I'm thinking about *going to the gym.*
    having a swim
    changing jobs
    taking a trip
    getting married

didn't do it yet

I've been meaning to *study.*
    repair this car
    stop smoking
    get in shape
    save some money

not thinking about

I can't get my mind *on school* lately.
    on these articles — about war
    off the war news thinking only.
    on working
    off improving my score (raise)

I've been trying to *call her* for the past few days.
    clean the house
    finish this paper
    get in touch with them to talk visit (contact)
    make a final decision — can't change, final

She's no doubt *talking to Joanne.*
    helping someone job - company.
    working on the presentation (in an office) information
    drinking coffee
sure.   *complaining about her job*

Your Turn

I. *idea can do*

Make some suggestions to your partner.

A: *Why don't you . . . ?*
B: *I've been trying to . . . .*
A: *How about . . . ?*
B: *I can't get my mind on . . . .*

join the band
study for the history exam
work harder
quit smoking

II. You have been trying to call some businesses for several days, but the line has always been busy. Tell your partner about this, and he or she will guess why the line has been so busy. Take turns calling these places.

the Opera House box office
Singapore Airlines
Macy's Department Store (NY)
City Hall
KQED Television Station
Sony
The Victoria and Albert Museum
New York Stock Exchange
The Pentagon

III. Use "always" to tell your partner about the habits of a few people who bother you or please you. He or she will answer with "no doubt" or "probably" and then try to explain the other person's behavior.

A: *My brother plays golf every day.*
B: *He's no doubt with business associates.* (partner)
A: *My husband always stays out late.*
B: *He's probably having a few drinks.*

your roommate
your father
the lady next door
the newsboy
your travel agent

Sharing

"Education is what we remember after we forget the things we learned in school." This saying emphasizes the role of education in shaping our ability to think. The purpose of study varies greatly according to level, country, and individual needs. All of us need to know the basic skills of reading, writing, and arithmetic, but higher education is broader. One purpose of education is to prepare us to do a job and make a living. Education in the international age teaches us to understand the world and to live and communicate with other people, even those who are quite different from us.

I. How are schools organized in your country? How many years must children attend school by law? Do most people in your country attend high school? How many people attend college or university? Is it difficult to enter universities where you live? Who pays for education? Are colleges expensive? Who can afford to go to college?

II. Do you enjoy studying and learning about new subjects? What was your favorite subject in elementary school? What is your favorite subject now? What kind of relationship do you have with your teachers? What would you change in your educational system?

III. Read and discuss the quotation about education at the top of this page. What is the role of facts in education? Are they important? When studying English for international communication, which is more important, correct grammar or willingness to make mistakes?

Try Your Hand

Read the following course descriptions and then write on the topics below.

ARCADIA UNIVERSITY

Philosophy 101 REFLECTIVE THINKING
Study of Plato's *Republic* and Aristotle's *Ethics*. How to study issues and values. Practice in discussing and debating.

History 301 AFRICAN-AMERICAN HISTORY
African origins. Slave trade. Resistance and rebellion. Underground Railroad. Emancipation Proclamation. Black Power Movement.

Music 201 MUSIC APPRECIATION
Highlights of Western music from the Middle Ages to the present. Influence of folk and ethnic music in Europe and America.

Economics 403 INTERNATIONAL BANKING
Comparison of banking systems througout the world. Influence of central banks on international fiscal policy. Role of the World Bank. Loans to developing countries.

Topic One
You want to take a course on the left. Write the teacher a letter explaining why.

Topic Two
Write a description and outline of a course about your home country and its culture.

Topic Three
Write a description of a course you would like to take but never had time for.

10 *Could you possibly help us?*

Conversation

Tom: Hi, Betty, how have you been?

Betty: Not so bad. How about you, Tom?

Tom: Well, Mike and I have a new apartment, and we're excited about moving on Saturday.

Betty: That's tomorrow! Gosh, you must be busy.

Tom: As a matter of fact, we are, and we have a lot more packing to do tonight. Listen, Betty, I know this is a lot to ask, but could you possibly give us a hand?

Betty: You mean with the moving tomorrow?

Tom: Uh-huh. We're really far behind and could use some help.

Betty: Sure, Tom. What time should I come over?

Tom: Let's see. We're going to rent a truck early in the morning, so could you possibly come at nine or so?

Betty: Sure, I'll get up early and come over after breakfast. But I usually sleep late on Saturday, so I wonder if you could give me a ring about eight or eight thirty just in case I oversleep.

Tom: Oh sure. I'll be glad to.

Betty: Great. I'd appreciate that. See you tomorrow.

Tom: Take care.

Betty: So long.

Variations

Gosh, you must be *busy.*
> *tired*
> *excited*
> *nervous*
> *worried*

Could you possibly *give us a hand?*
> *lend me ten dollars* — give me (he gives)
> *help us with the packing*
> *let me borrow your car* — want to take, (and pay back)
> *call me tomorrow night*

We could use *some help.*
> *a hand*
> *some free time*
> *a little relaxation later*
> *a nice dinner*

What time should I *come over?*
> *call you*
> *get up*
> *leave the house*
> *meet you*

I wonder if you could *give me a ring.*
> *tell me where the post office is*
> *help us with the move tomorrow*
> *turn down your stereo*
> *get me another beer*

would

I'd appreciate *that.*
> *a call tomorrow morning*
> *hearing from you* (call, visit family)
> *some help*
> *your giving us a hand* (helping)

Your Turn

I. **Ask your partner to lend you the following things:**

his/her car
a dictionary
his/her Walkman
a hundred dollars
a book on Hong Kong
his/her skis
a camera
an eraser
a bicycle

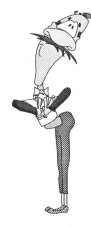

II. **Give a good reason or explanation and then ask your partner to:**

help you move
give you a hand with your English homework
call you tomorrow at 8:00
tell your English teacher you are sick
help you find an apartment
buy you a drink since you are broke
speak a little more slowly
go with you to the doctor
buy you a ticket to the Madonna concert
stop blowing smoke in your face

III. **Tell your partner what you think using "you must be":**

A: I worked till 2:00 a.m. yesterday.
B: You must be <u>tired</u>.
A: As a matter of fact, I am.

I haven't eaten anything since breakfast.
Tomorrow my vacation starts.
My cat died yesterday.
I'm taking my exams next week.
My son made the honor roll in school.
I got a big raise in salary.
I had to cancel my trip abroad.
His wife baked a cake for me.
My boss called me at 2:00 a.m.

Sharing

Asking someone to do you a favor is an essential social skill. When you ask for favors in English, it is important to use language that tells other people you care about their feelings. This is why expressions such as "I wonder if . . ." and "Could you possibly . . ." are so useful. Quite often the language you use to ask favors changes and becomes more polite and indirect depending on how great the favor is and how inconvenient it is to the other person.

I. In your native language, how do you ask people for favors? What is important to remember when you do this? Are there any differences in English? Talk about some of them.

II. Have you ever asked someone to do something special for you? What was it? How did you feel asking for it? Describe the situation. How do you feel when someone asks you for a favor? What was the most difficult thing you ever asked someone for? Who did you ask?

III. When someone asks for a favor, what are some ways to say "yes" in English? How can you say "no" politely when someone asks you to do something you don't want to or can't do? Are there any general, universally accepted rules for giving and receiving favors? Is indirect language sometimes problematical? When communicating internationally, what is the best rule of thumb?

Try Your Hand

Read the following letter and then write on the topics below.

Dear Tom,

How are things with you? I have been busy studying for my classes and haven't had time to write. You must be busy, too, with your studies.

How do you and Mike like your new apartment? Have you had a big house-warming party yet?

By the way, I am coming to visit next month and could use a place to stay. I was wondering if I could stay with you? I'd really appreciate it. If that's o.k., let me know as soon as you can. Also, could you or Mike possibly meet me at the airport?

I'm really looking forward to seeing your new place and to visiting your campus.

As ever,

Bart

Topic One
Write a letter to a friend asking to borrow some money. Give a good reason.

Topic Two
Write a short note asking a friend to lend you his truck. You are moving next week.

Topic Three
Write a note replying to Bart's letter here on the left.

What time did you get here?

Conversation

Pedro: I'm sorry to be so late. Have you been waiting long?

Mayumi: Not really. *waiting a little, ok.*

Pedro: I hope you're not upset with me. What time did you get here?

Mayumi: About quarter to two, and it's only quarter after two now. I wonder what happened to the others.

Pedro: They must be running late, too. *(logical)*

Mayumi: The concert starts at three o'clock sharp, *(exactly)* so I hope they arrive before too long. *(soon)*

Pedro: I'm hardly ever late, but yesterday I had to work overtime. I seldom do. *(never)* *same*

Mayumi: What time do you usually get off work? *finish*

Pedro: Well, the restaurant closes at midnight,

and I'm always at home by 12:30 or so, *(about)*

but last night we didn't close until 12:25.

Mayumi: Oh look. Here they come now.

Joanne: We're sorry to keep you waiting.

The car wouldn't start and we

had to take a taxi.

Mike: I really apologize. *(very)*

The car rarely breaks down. *seldom*

Mayumi: Don't worry about it.

We have plenty of time. *a lot*

Variations

I'm sorry *to be so late.*
> *to keep you waiting*
> *for being so late*
> *I kept you waiting*
> *I'm not on time*

Have you been waiting long? *Not really.*
> *not exactly*
> *actually, no*
> *I guess not*
> *well, no*

I hope you're not *upset with* me.
> *angry with*
> *irritated with*
> *furious with*
> *mad at*

I'm *hardly ever* late.
> *almost never*
> *rarely*
> *seldom*
> *usually not*

He *usually* gets off work *at midnight.*
> *sometimes . . . late*
> *frequently . . . early*
> *always . . . on time*
> *never . . . at noon*

He always gets home by *12:30* or so.
> *6:15*
> *9:45*
> *11:15*
> *10:30*

Lesson Eleven **43**

Your Turn

I. Tell your partner about your daily routine. What do you usually do and not do every day? Be as specific as possible. Use some of the following words:

always
usually
never
sometimes
infrequently
rarely
seldom
almost never
almost always

II. Find out about your partner's daily time schedule. What time does he or she:

get up
go to bed
have breakfast (lunch, dinner)
study
exercise
go to meetings
leave for school or work
get home at night
take a coffee/tea break
have a snack

III. You have kept your partner waiting. Apologize and explain why you were late. Here are some reasons you can use:

my car broke down
the bus was late
I had a last-minute phone call
I had to work overtime
the traffic was heavy
my sister was sick
I got out of class late
I was at the doctor's office
I had a hangover
I overslept

Sharing

People from different cultures around the world treat time differently. In Latin America, it is not considered impolite to be late for an appointment, but in America and Europe, punctuality is important. If you are late for an appointment, even with a casual friend, it is necessary to apologize to the person you have kept waiting. It is an interesting contradiction that people in English-speaking countries are usually on time for appointments, but when telling time they are often vague: "about noon," "four thirty or so," "sixish." (about 6)

I. Discuss with your classmates how people in your country feel about time. Is it important to be "on time"? What does being "late" mean? What happens if you are late for an appointment? How long do you wait for someone before you leave?

II. Have you ever been very late for an appointment? Why were you late and how did you explain it? Have you ever waited for someone who was extremely late for an appointment? What kinds of thoughts did you have while you were waiting? What would you say to a friend who is always late and keeps you waiting?

III. "Information anxiety" and "hurry sickness" are caused by the overload of new ideas and the pressure of rushing to follow a hectic schedule. What do you think the solution for stress is? How can we cope with our responsibilities and still remain healthy?

Try Your Hand

Read the following schedule and then write on the topics below.

International Conference on Cross-Cultural Communication
Schedule

7:00 A.M.	Wake-Up Call
7:30	Breakfast
8:30	Morning Lecture
10:30	Group Discussion
12:00 Noon	Lunch
1:30	Afternoon Lecture
3:30	Workshop
5:00	Free Time
6:30	Dinner
8:00	Evening Program
9:30	Free Time
12:00 Midnight	Lights Out

Topic One
You are attending the conference on the left. Write to your boss about it.

Topic Two
The conference sponsors want comments. Write a note about the terrible food.

Topic Three
Write out a schedule for a one-day conference on any theme you choose.

How's the weather?

Conversation

Pedro: We've had two weeks of bad weather.

Tom: Yes, we've had a lot of rain this year, but don't worry, we usually have pleasant weather in the spring.

Mayumi: I'm looking forward to going to the beach this summer.

want (because it's nice)
preposition

Pedro: Me, too. I love warm weather.

Mayumi: What's the weather like where you're from, Pedro?

Pedro: Well, in Mexico the summers are usually quite hot and humid, but you get used to it.

very   *moisture, wet*
comfortable, OK

Tom: How's the weather in Japan, Mayumi?

Mayumi: It snows a lot in the north, and it's cold and windy, but in the south, the climate is tropical, always bright and sunny. It reminds you of Hawaii.

think

Pedro: What's the weather going to be like tomorrow, Tom?

Tom: The forecast on television said cool and cloudy, but only a slight chance of rain.

little (10%)   possibility

Mayumi: Oh, good. I hope it clears off for the weekend. I've made plans to play tennis.

will be nice

Pedro: I hope so, too. We could use some nice weather.

want

Variations

We've had *two weeks of bad weather.*

> *a lot of rain this spring*
>
> 3 - 5   *several days of beautiful weather*
>
> *nice weather all summer*
>
> *too much snow this year*

Don't worry, *we usually have a pleasant spring.*

> *it never rains*
>
> *the summers are always sunny*
>
> *it's rarely foggy* (a) *hardly ever, almost never*
>
> *the fall is beautiful*

What's the weather like **where you're from?**

> *how's the weather*
>
> *what's the climate like*
>
> *what kind of weather do you have*
>
> *what are the summers like*

In the *north,* **it's usually** *cold and windy.*

> *southwest . . . warm and sunny*
>
> *east . . . cloudy and rainy*
>
> *south . . . hot and humid*
>
> *west . . . mild and pleasant*
>
> /middle

I've made plans to *play tennis.*

> *go to the museum*
>
> go to   *leave for New York*
>
> *visit my mother*
>
> *spend the day at the beach*

need (would like)

We could use *some nice weather.*

> *some more rain*
>
> *a little less fog* (n)
>
> *a few sunny days*
>
> *a few days of cool weather*

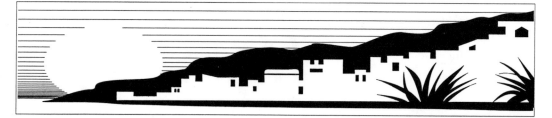

Your Turn

I.   Here is the weather forecast of some Asian cities. You and your partner are planning a trip to Asia. Ask each other about the weather.

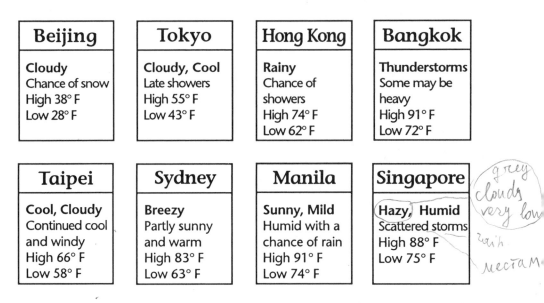

Beijing	**Tokyo**	**Hong Kong**	**Bangkok**
Cloudy	Cloudy, Cool	Rainy	Thunderstorms
Chance of snow	Late showers	Chance of	Some may be
High 38° F	High 55° F	showers	heavy
Low 28° F	Low 43° F	High 74° F	High 91° F
		Low 62° F	Low 72° F

Taipei	**Sydney**	**Manila**	**Singapore**
Cool, Cloudy	Breezy	Sunny, Mild	Hazy, Humid
Continued cool	Partly sunny	Humid with a	Scattered storms
and windy	and warm	chance of rain	High 88° F
High 66° F	High 83° F	High 91° F	Low 75° F
Low 58° F	Low 63° F	Low 74° F	

(handwritten: grey clouds very low rain nectam)

II. Tell your partner about what the weather is like in your country. Ask what it is like in your partner's hometown.

III. You are making plans for the near future. Tell your partner about them and ask about the weather. Here are some suggestions. Add your own also.

Suggested Language:
A. I've made plans to . . . .
B. Don't worry . . . .
A. I'm planning to . . . .
B. I'm afraid . . . .

Things to do:
go jogging
have a picnic
play baseball
go to the beach
repair your roof
go fishing
take a hike

Sharing

Everybody talks about the weather. Whether we are chatting with old friends or people we have just met, the weather is perhaps the most popular subject of small talk the world over. Why is this so? First, the weather is something we all share in common. Second, the weather is a fairly safe and non-controversial subject (global warming and the destruction of the ozone layer are more problematical). Finally, weather talk can easily lead to further conversation topics. In any case, when in doubt, you can always talk about the weather, so it pays to know some expressions in English to cover this topic essential for international communication.

I. In Eskimo languages there are many different words for "snow." Are there any interesting words to describe the weather in your native language? Does your country have four seasons? Are there any special rainy, windy or dry periods?

II. Do you watch the weather news on television? How is it presented? How do you like the climate where you live? Share with your classmates how you feel when the weather changes unexpectedly and ruins your plans.

III. Some scientists believe the world's weather is changing because of air pollution. If this is true, what do you feel can be done? Discuss the issue with your classmates. Do you think there should be an international agency to prevent pollution of the environment?

Try Your Hand

Read the following letter and then write on the topics below.

Waikiki Beach
February 23

Dear Ruth,
    We're having a wonderful time in Hawaii. The weather today is fabulous. Sunny, but not too humid, and just a little windy in the afternoon. We were able to spend all morning at the beach.
    Yesterday it rained for a few minutes, but it has been dry ever since. Tomorrow we leave for Beijing, and they expect snow and ice there for the next week. See you next month.
            Yours,
            Barbara

Topic One
Drop a note to some friends about the weather today.

Topic Two
Describe the worst weather you have ever experienced.

Topic Three
Friends from abroad are visiting. Write them about what the weather will be like.

Are you going to get a job?

Conversation

Joanne: When is your birthday, Mayumi?

Mayumi: It's August the eighteenth. When's yours?

Joanne: February the twelfth. I'll soon be twenty-one.
Do you mind if I ask how old you are?

Mayumi: No, that's all right. I just turned twenty-two.

Joanne: We're almost the same age.

Mayumi: Have you ever wondered what your future will be like?

Joanne: Every now and then I think about it, yes.

Mayumi: Are you going to get a job?

Joanne: Possibly, but I'm planning to go to graduate school first.

Do you think you'll have a career?

Mayumi: I haven't made up my mind about that yet,

but I've thought about international business.

Joanne: That's going to be an important

field in the next few years.

You'll be rich and famous.

Mayumi: I hope I will,

but I don't think so.

Joanne: Well, you never know.

Variations

Do you mind *if I ask how old you are?*
        telling me your age
        if I invite Tom
        staying a while longer
        not having dessert today — *désert — nycтошин*

Have you ever wondered *what your future will be like?*
        where you will be in twenty years
        who will be the next Prime Minister
        why dogs wag their tails (wagged)
        how much time it takes to learn karate

Every now and then *I think about my future.*
        my brother visits me
        we go skiing
        there is a good program on television
        she reads a short story

to future

I'm planning to *go to graduate school.*
        visit Scotland next year
        buy a house in the country
talk   *chat with my mother*
        work next year

I haven't made up my mind about *a career* **yet.**
        the writing project
        studying economics
        Dr. Lee (my opinion about.
        going to the concert

I hope *I'll be rich and famous.*
        you'll come to see me in Italy post
        I get a big raise in salary
        we can meet in Bangkok
        I pass the entrance exams

Your Turn

I. You are the sales representative for a model agency. Your partner is a customer looking for some models for a commercial. Tell him everything you can about these models. The customer will ask you questions also.

Bessie
Age—21
Height—5' 2"
Weight—120 lbs.

☆☆ Very talented and cute
Can dance and sing
Wants to make a record
★★ Very shy
No experience being photographed

Jerry
Age—44
Height—6' 2"
Weight—160 lbs.

☆☆ Dashing, continental appearance
Popular among middle-aged women
Did a popular commercial last year
★★ Younger people don't like him
Heavy drinker

Lilly
Age—32
Height—5'
Weight—110 lbs.

☆☆ Glamorous
Very well-known
Star of several movies
★★ Has had several quarrels with directors
Often late for rehearsal; temperamental

Brad
Age—28
Height—6'
Weight—155 lbs.

☆☆ Handsome and masculine
Very professional
Star of a TV series
★★ Fee is extremely high
No experience doing commercials

II. Have a conversation with your partner about what you have done in the past and what you have been doing recently. Then talk about what you might like to do in the immediate future. Alternate roles.

Suggested Language:
Have you ever . . . ?
Every now and then . . . .
I've thought about . . . .
I'm planning to . . . .

III. Talk to your partner about the distant future. What are your goals and ambitions? What do you hope to be doing in ten years? Twenty years? Be imaginative. Your partner should make comments and ask you some questions. Switch roles.

Sharing

"What do you do?" This is a common question in casual conversation, and it is understandable why we ask it. Knowing what people do can tell us something about them or at least about how they spend much of their time. Also, many people strongly identify with their occupation or with the company they work for. While this simple inquiry can possibly lead to further conversation, the timing and suitability of the question are not always clear. Some cultures see questions about work and age as too personal and even rude.

I. Do people talk about their jobs a lot in your country? Is it O. K. to ask a person you have just met what their job is? Do certain jobs have more prestige than others? Discuss the highest and lowest types of work in your society. What determines prestige or recognition in a job?

II. Are you working now? Are you a full-time student? Do you like what you are doing? How would you like to change it? Do you want to imitate your parents' lifestyle? Why? Why not?

III. In past times, people lived in the same town and did the same job all their lives. Nowadays, they often work in foreign countries. Why are so many leaving home to work in other countries? Discuss this with your classmates. What are the problems involved for the countries with "guest workers" and for the workers themselves who leave home?

Try Your Hand

Read the following resumé and then write on the topics below.

Resumé

Roger N. Sanchez
1042 Greenlaw Ave.
San Jose, California 95101
TEL. 408-932-7654

Career Objective:
To work in international sales for a major computer manufacturer

Education:
B. A. San Jose State University, 1991
Major: International Business

Experience:
Part-time salesclerk at Computer Wonderland, San Jose, 1987-present

Special Skills:
Programming in C and Pascal
Fluent German; Conversational Japanese

Hobbies and Interests:
Swimming, historical novels, science fiction, movies

Topic One
You are Roger Sanchez. Write to Trans World Computers, Inc. about a job.

Topic Two
Describe your ideal job and what you will do at the job.

Topic Three
Using the resumé on the left as a guide, write your own resumé.

14 When does your flight leave?

Conversation

Pedro: Do you have any plans for summer vacation, Mayumi?

Mayumi: Yes, I'm going to take a trip to Canada. Have you ever been there?

Pedro: No, I haven't, but they say it's a beautiful country. Isn't the capital Montreal?

Mayumi: No, I believe it's Ottawa.

Pedro: Oh, that's right. They speak French in Canada, don't they?

Mayumi: Many people do, especially in Quebec.

Pedro: Are you flying?

Mayumi: Yes, I've already made reservations.

Pedro: When does your flight leave?

Mayumi: June the fifteenth.

Pedro: And how long are you staying there?

Mayumi: About two weeks. It's a special budget tour.

Pedro: It'll probably be a great trip.
I'd like to see the whole world someday.

Mayumi: Me, too. Let's go together.

Variations

Do you have any plans for *summer vacation?*
     the Christmas holidays
     your birthday
     this coming Sunday
     the weekend

Have you ever been to *Canada?*
     Australia
     the Caribbean
     Eastern Europe
     the Metropolitan Museum

I believe it's *Ottawa.*
     the building next door
     about an hour's drive from here
     an interesting city
     getting late

Are you *flying?*
     driving
     taking the bus
     going by train
     walking

I've already *made reservations.*
     charged it to my credit card
     written to the hotel
     rented a car for two weeks
     been to Brisbane

It'll probably be *a great trip.*
     cool there in the summer
     an exciting vacation
     tomorrow before I can finish
     late when I get home

Your Turn

I.   Have you ever taken a trip? Tell your partner about it. Where did you go? How did you get there? Where did you stay? For how long? What did you see? Did anything exciting happen? Did you have any bad experiences? Would you recommend the trip to someone else? What words of caution *Be careful* would you give to someone going there?

II. You and your partner are in charge of planning a three-day outing for your class to a place not more than an hour's travel time away. Decide where you are going to go and then outline a time schedule for the trip, showing the activities for each day.

III. Ask your partner about the capital of various countries. Then suggest the language spoken there.

A: What's the capital of Canada?
B: I believe it's Ottawa, isn't it?
A: They speak French in Canada, don't they?
B: I think so./I'm not sure . . . .

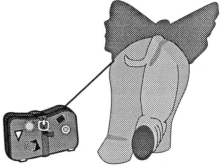

France	*Liberia*
Algeria	*India*
Peru	*Israel*
Egypt	*New Zealand*
Norway	*Brazil*
Australia	*China*
Singapore	*Kenya*
Romania	*Saudi Arabia*
Holland	*South Africa*
Japan	*Portugal*

IV. Now, you and your partner should make your own list of countries, their capitals, and the languages spoken there. Share the list with the class.

V.   Quiz your partner about famous places.

Which country is famous for _____?
Where is _____?
Do you know where _____ is?

Sharing

The Global Village has become reality. Transportation and telecommunications networks have brought us all together in ways that we never imagined. English is the linguistic cement that binds together much of the world. Airline pilots on international flights communicate with ground control in English. Wherever you land in the world, you can assume that the customs and immigration officials can speak at least some English. Travel agents all over the globe usually speak English. As the international language, English is no longer the possession merely of its native speakers; it belongs to the global community.

I. What kind of transportation do people use most frequently in your country? Autos? Buses? Trains? Is there a national airline? Are there private airlines? What is the travel industry like in your country?

II. Where have you travelled? Do you prefer to travel in groups or individually? What travel plans do you have for the future? If you could, would you take a trip into space?

III. There is an old saying that "travel broadens." Is this true? Why do most of us still experience "culture shock" when we go to a different country? What do you know about culture shock? Why is it a problem? Do you think it will go away as an international consciousness develops?

Try Your Hand

Read the following itinerary and then write on the topics below.

Whirlwind Tours
EUROPE IN A WEEK
Itinerary

Sunday–London:	Buckingham Palace; The Tower; St. Paul's
Monday–Paris:	Eiffel Tower; Arc de Triomphe; Notre Dame
Tuesday–Brussels:	EEC Headquarters
Wednesday–Munich:	Cathedral; Hofbräuhaus
Thursday–Milan:	La Scala; Il Duomo; Designer Boutiques
Friday–Rome:	Coliseum; Vatican; Spanish Steps
Saturday–Athens:	Acropolis; Parthenon
Sunday–Istanbul:	Santa Sophia; Topkapi Museum

Topic One
Write a letter to a friend about the tour on the left which you went on.

Topic Two
Write a note to Whirlwind Tours thanking them for the excellent tour you went on.

Topic Three
Make out an itinerary for your tour of a lifetime.

15 *Something strange happened.*

Conversation

Tom: Something strange happened to me last night when I was leaving work.

Betty: Oh, really. What?

Tom: I had just left the Café Formidable and was about to get into my car when a man walked up and asked me a question.

Betty: What's so strange about that?

Tom: Well, he was wearing a bright yellow clown suit with green polka dots. He had huge red shoes and was carrying a bunch of balloons.

Betty: You're kidding! You must have been surprised.

Tom: I was. In fact, I was amazed.

Betty: Did he say anything to you?

Tom: He said he had been trying to find the Hilton Hotel and had gotten lost.

Betty: Why was he looking for the Hilton?

Tom: He told me they were having a big party there for the Save the Animals Foundation.

Betty: And it was a costume party. Right?

Tom: Exactly! How did you know?

Betty: I just guessed.

Variations

He was *leaving work.*
    going home
    talking with a stranger
    driving home
    flying to Milan

I had just *left the restaurant.*
    taken the driving test
    put my coat on
    gotten up
    finished working

He was about to *get into his car.*
    cross the street
    have another coffee
    leave home
    say something

He had red shoes. *You're kidding!*
    I don't believe it
    I'm amazed
    no kidding
    you can't be serious

You must have been *surprised.*
    excited
    scared
    lucky
    mistaken

It was a costume party. *Right?*
    wasn't it
    don't you think
    isn't that so
    huh

Come as You Are!

Your Turn

I. Tell your partner about an unforgettable experience; something strange, funny, inspiring, unusual, or anything you would like to talk about. Your partner will ask you questions to clear up details. Change roles.

II. Here are four short stories. Choose one or two of them and tell it to your partner as if you experienced it or as if a friend of yours did. Your partner will do the same with different stories from the ones you chose.

1. Marie is a waitress in an expensive French restaurant. One day she gets a reservation for two people who ask to be served the best champagne and caviar. When they come, Marie is surprised. They are a famous Prince and Princess who are in the news a lot. She is so nervous that when she serves the soup, she spills some of it on the Princess's skirt. She is terribly embarrassed and apologizes. The Princess smiles, says that's O. K., and they chat with her about the restaurant business.

2. Linda is an actress who has very poor eyesight. One day she is at home getting ready to go to work and is putting on her makeup. She can't find her glasses, but she is late, so she does the best she can. She goes to the television station to be interviewed, but when she walks into the studio the announcer takes one look at her face and starts laughing. Linda is furious, but when she looks in the mirror, she knows why he is laughing. She tells him what happened, and they both laugh together.

3. Greg has a stomach ulcer and his doctor says he should not eat spicy foods or drink alcohol. He doesn't like to tell people about his ulcer. His new girlfriend Martha comes over to his place and cooks dinner. She serves Mexican food—tacos, enchiladas, salsa, and tequila. He hardly eats or drinks anything. She is very upset, starts crying, and leaves the house while Greg answers the phone. The next day, he calls her and tells her about his ulcer. They make up and plan to eat at a Cantonese restaurant.

4. Leslie, a jeweler, gets a call asking him to come to a hotel room downtown for a special conference. When he arrives, a man in a black suit shows him the largest uncut diamond he has ever seen. The man wants him to cut it into a necklace for someone. But the jeweler must tell no one about it. Leslie agrees, and after two months he delivers the finished necklace. It is so beautiful, the man pays him twice what he promised to pay. The next day, Leslie reads in the paper that two months ago, the world's largest uncut diamond was stolen.

Sharing

Clothes say a lot about who we are. It may not be completely true that "clothes make the man," but people often judge us by the way we dress. Advertising and journalism use the term "fashion statement." This means that we "say" something with our clothes; they express our personality and tastes. Western clothing has become popular everywhere in the world, but in Asia, the Middle East, Africa, and other areas, one still can see traditional clothing worn on the street. Nowadays, however, jeans and running shoes seem to be the uniform for young people in every country.

I. What kind of clothing do most people wear in your homeland? Is there a traditional dress? Who wears it and when do they wear it? Does clothing have any social significance in your country? Can you tell the rich from the poor by looking at their clothing?

II. Have you ever worn traditional clothing that is characteristic of your country? Have you ever gone to a costume party? What did you wear? Share with your group what your favorite clothing is.

III. Western clothing is worn in most countries, and traditional costumes and dress are gradually disappearing. Do you think this is a harmful tendency? Share your feelings and ideas about clothes and fashions with your classmates.

Try Your Hand

Read the following story and then write on the topics below.

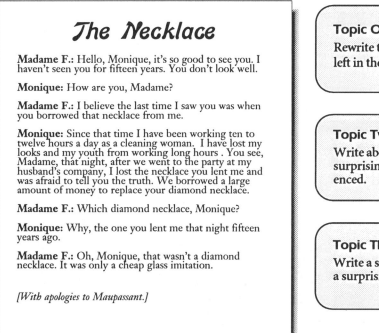

The Necklace

Madame F.: Hello, Monique, it's so good to see you. I haven't seen you for fifteen years. You don't look well.

Monique: How are you, Madame?

Madame F.: I believe the last time I saw you was when you borrowed that necklace from me.

Monique: Since that time I have been working ten to twelve hours a day as a cleaning woman. I have lost my looks and my youth from working long hours. You see, Madame, that night, after we went to the party at my husband's company, I lost the necklace you lent me and was afraid to tell you the truth. We borrowed a large amount of money to replace your diamond necklace.

Madame F.: Which diamond necklace, Monique?

Monique: Why, the one you lent me that night fifteen years ago.

Madame F.: Oh, Monique, that wasn't a diamond necklace. It was only a cheap glass imitation.

[With apologies to Maupassant.]

Topic One
Rewrite the short drama on the left in the form of a story.

Topic Two
Write about something surprising that you experienced.

Topic Three
Write a short, short story with a surprising twist at the end.

16   *If I had a million dollars . . .*

Conversation

Mike: What would you do if somebody gave you a million dollars, Tom?

Tom: A million dollars? Wow! If I had a million dollars now, I would travel.

Pedro: Where do you think you would go?

Tom: Hmm. That's a difficult question. Let me think about it. I'd like to see the Eiffel Tower in Paris, the bullfights in Madrid, the pyramids in Egypt, and the Kremlin in Moscow. Gee, there are so many fascinating places. I guess I'd just go around the world and see all the sights.

Pedro: How about you, Mike?

Mike: I'm not all that fond of travelling, but if I were, I'd want to go to someplace exotic like Nepal.

Tom: What would you do if you had a lot of money, Pedro?

Pedro: Oh, that's easy, I'd buy twelve sports cars.

Mike: Why twelve?

Pedro: A different one for each month of the year.

Variations

If I had *a million dollars* **now, I would** *travel.*
>> *more time . . . study Portuguese*
>> *the down payment . . . buy a house*
>> *a better job . . . make more money*
>> *a camera . . . take some pictures*

Where **do you think you would** *go?*
>> *what . . . buy*
>> *who . . . visit*
>> *how much . . . spend*
>> *when . . . leave*

Hmm. That's *a difficult question.*
>> *an interesting question*
>> *hard to answer*
>> *something I never thought about*
>> *not easy to say*

I *guess* **I'd just** *go around the world.*
>> *suppose . . . visit Paris*
>> *imagine . . . take a long vacation*
>> *think . . . eat in the best restaurants*
>> *have an idea . . . do nothing*

I'm not all that fond of *travelling.*
>> *playing tennis*
>> *washing dishes*
>> *pets*
>> *her father*

If he were *interested in travel,* **he would** *go to Nepal.*
>> *taller . . . play basketball*
>> *better at math . . . study physics*
>> *not so lazy . . . get up earlier*
>> *my friend . . . lend me his car*

Your Turn

I. What would you do if you had a million dollars now? Share your fantasy with your partner and then switch roles. Explain in detail. Tell why and how you would do it.

    Some language suggestions:
    If I had . . . I would . . . .
    If I had . . . I guess I'd . . . .

II. Let your imagination go where it wants to go. What if you could be another person? Who would you be? What would you do? Here are some suggestions. Feel free to come up with other people.

    the Queen of England
    the head of your country
    a famous musician
    the President of the United States
    your next door neighbor
    a Nobel Prize winning scientist
    a world champion athlete
    your English teacher
    a journalist

III. Talk about the following situations. Say what you would do if they were so:

    Someone asks you to kill another person for money—a lot of money.
    Your boss offers you a promotion, but says you will not get a raise.
    You win a free trip to Bali.
    You find out you have AIDS and have one year to live.
    Your brother just wrecked your new car.
    Hollywood wants you to star in the next Rambo movie.
    Your spouse is having an affair and you find out about it.
    A high school counsellor tells you your son has a drug problem.
    You can have a date with any film star you choose.

Sharing

Mahatma Gandhi once said: "If I had no sense of humor, I would long ago have committed suicide." Most people would agree that laughing is healthy, and yet various cultures find different things funny. Some humor crosses cultural boundaries, but jokes and stories that are humorous in one culture sometimes seem strange in another. One reason for this is that humor often relies on shared experience or cultural information that may not be universal. Frequently, when we hear jokes from another culture, they don't seem funny to us.

I. What kind of humor is typical in your country? Can you think of some jokes that everybody in your homeland might know? Share them with the class and see if people find them funny or not. Don't be too surprised if you need to explain why they are funny.

II. Do you like jokes? Tell a few to the class. What is your favorite funny story? Share it with your classmates. Can you think of a humorous movie that you have seen recently? Why was it so amusing?

III. Can animals laugh? We know that many animals feel pain and grief if one of their group dies, but do they have a sense of humor similar to humans? Is humor something that only humans can share? If humor is a universal human characteristic, how can we use it to further international understanding?

Try Your Hand

Read the following and then write on the topics below.

Have A Laugh!

A woman sitting at the bar had drunk too much, and the bartender said she couldn't have another drink. She was very angry and said: "If I were your wife, I would put poison in your coffee." The bartender answered: "Madam, if you were my wife, I would drink it."

Yesterday I was chatting with the mayor at City Hall about the new city office building. Since the building was over 30 stories tall, I asked her how many people worked there. "Well," she said, "just about half of them. The others just draw their salaries."

 How many English teachers does it take to change a light bulb? Three. Why three? One to pronounce the name of the brand correctly, another to make you repeat it ten times, and a third to give you a grade.

Topic One
Write down in English a joke that you know.

Topic Two
Write about the funniest thing that ever happened to you.

Topic Three
Describe the most amusing person you have ever known.

In my opinion . . .

Conversation

Pedro: Joanne, do you think a woman should be president of the United States?

Joanne: In my opinion, it should have happened a long time ago. Don't you think so, Mayumi?

Mayumi: I agree. I believe a woman could be a great president. How do you feel about that, Mike?

Mike: Well, to be perfectly honest, I disagree. I think children need mothers at home.

Joanne: You have a point there, Mike, but not all women want to be housewives. Tell me—would you like to stay at home every day and not have any career choices?

Mike: Now that you mention it, probably not, but would you want to be told you must have a political career and can't have a family?

Joanne: If you put it that way, I don't think so.

Pedro: That's why childcare is such an important issue today.

Mayumi: You're absolutely right, Pedro. I couldn't agree more.

Mike: I'm still not convinced.

Variations

In my opinion, *a woman should be president.*
>   *television is getting worse*
>   *football is exciting*
>   *children need attention*
>   *drugs are dangerous*

How do you feel **about that, Mike?**
>   *what do you think*
>   *what do you have to say*
>   *what's your opinion*
>   *do you have any thoughts*

Well, to be perfectly honest, *I disagree.*
>   *I don't see it that way*
>   *my view is a little different*
>   *I have another opinion*
>   *I'm not sure I agree*

Now that you mention it, *probably not.*
>   *I guess not*
>   *I'm really not sure*
>   *I can't say for sure*
>   *I can't decide*

If you put it that way, *I don't think so.*
>   *I doubt it*
>   *definitely not*
>   *not on your life*
>   *not a chance*

You're absolutely right. *I couldn't agree more.*
>   *my feelings exactly*
>   *I completely agree*
>   *I couldn't have said it better*
>   *you hit the nail on the head*

Your Turn

I. Partner A states the following opinions. Partner B agrees or disagrees. Take turns. Then express some opinions of your own.

Dieting is good for you.
I hate classical music.
Television is for idiots.
The Cold War is over.
Money is the root of all evil.

II. Discuss the following topics with your partner or in a small group. If you are in favor of the subject (the "pro" side), state your views. If you disagree with the subject (the "con" side), use the proper language and speak against the topic. Remember that some of these topics are controversial. Many people will have strong opinions, both pro and con.

Women who do the same work as men should get the same pay.
Human beings are destroying the environment.
Animals should be used for medical experiments.
The United Nations is important for keeping peace in the world.
English should not be the international language.
People who kill others should be punished by death (the "death penalty").
War is always bad.

III. Choose sides and discuss these four situations. The pro side will speak in favor of the topic, the con side will take the opposite point of view.

1—Country A wants to export wheat, but the farmers in country B think the competition will destroy their farming industry. What should each country do?

2—Foreigners living in country Q think they should be able to vote in the national elections. The government of country Q says "no." Who is right?

3—Students at X High School are not allowed to have long hair. The teachers say long hair makes a bad impression and hurts the school. Some students disagree and want to wear their hair long. Should the school change its rules?

4—There is a war going in a distant place. The government of country C wants to send doctors and nurses to help take care of wounded civilians. Several hospitals in country C say that if the doctors and nurses volunteer they will lose their jobs. What should the government do?

Sharing

Major social changes are taking place all over the world, and English is changing as a result. Black people in the United States were once called "Negroes," but they disliked that term, and many now want to be called "Blacks" or "African-Americans." Feminism has also changed the language. Many females now prefer Ms. to Miss or Mrs., and "woman" to "lady" or "girl." Many homosexual people describe themselves with the word "gay," and many individuals with physical problems prefer to be called "disabled" rather than "handicapped."

I. Has your native language changed much recently because of social changes in your culture? Is there a women's liberation movement in your country? Are there other liberation movements? Has English had any effect on language used for women or minority groups in your country?

II. How do you feel about feminism? Do you think men and women should have different social roles?

III. How do you feel about changes in attitudes towards women and women's roles in society? What do you think the long-term international effect of feminism will be? What about other liberation movements? Can you foresee any problems in relations between people from different cultures as a result of these social changes?

Try Your Hand

Study the following list and then write on the topics below.

Changing English

OLD TERM	NEW TERM
Chairman	Chairperson
Deaf	Hearing-Impaired
Dumb	Speech-Impaired
Fireman	Firefighter
Gluttony	Eating Disorder
Handicapped	Disabled
Homosexual	Gay
Illegal Alien	Undocumented Worker
Lady/Girl	Woman
Miss/Mrs.	Ms.
Negro	Black/African-American
Policeman	Police Officer
Retarded Children	Exceptional Children
Stewardess	Flight Attendant
Wife/Husband	Significant Other/Partner

Topic One
Would you feel comfortable using the new terms listed? Uncomfortable using them? Which ones? Why?

Topic Two
Do you think that using these new terms will change the way we think? Explain.

Topic Three
Choose a few of the terms listed on the left and discuss them.

18

I'd like the steak, please.

Conversation

Mike: A table for two, please.

Waiter: I believe we have one free next to the window.

Right this way, please. May I get you something to drink?

Mike: We'd like to take a look at the menu first.

What do you feel like having, Betty?

Betty: I think I'll have the steak.

Mike: I'm going to have the roast beef.

Waiter: May I take your order?

Betty: Yes, I'd like the steak, please.

Waiter: How would you like your steak cooked?

Betty: Medium, please.

Mike: I'll have the roast beef, rare.

Waiter: And would you care for wine?

Mike: I guess we'll have the house wine

and some coffee after dinner.

(*The food arrives*)

Betty: Wow, this steak really looks good.

Mike: I'll say! So does the roast beef,

and I'm really starving, too.

Variations

I believe *we have a free table.*
he's coming tomorrow
the concert starts at eight
we have time for dessert
Joanne went home early

We'd like to take a look at *the menu.*
the dessert tray
the wine list
next week's schedule
the new library

May I *take your order?*
suggest our house special
offer you some more wine
help you with that
take your coat

I'd like *the steak,* **please.**
the seafood special
to order some wine
to try the shish-kebab
a cocktail

Would you care *for wine?*
to try the chocolate mousse
for more coffee
to have dinner in your room
for something to drink

I guess *we'll have coffee later.*
you're tired of studying
I'll try the French onion soup
your roommate won't be here
the waiter forgot our order

Your Turn

I. Ask your partner the following questions, then switch roles. When answering, use "I guess," "I believe," and "I think."

Would you like a table for two?
May I get you something to drink?
May I take your order?
How would you like your eggs?
Would you like soup or salad?
Would you care for wine with your meal?
Would you care for dessert later?
May I offer you some more coffee?
How would you like your steak cooked?
Do you care for cream with your coffee?

II. Using the items below, practice ordering several different meals from your partner, who will play the waiter or waitress. Switch roles.

Tomato Soup
Bean Soup
Shrimp Cocktail
Hamburger
French Fries
Cheese Omelet
Meat Loaf
Mixed Vegetables
Baked Potato
Caesar Salad
Apple Pie
Ice Cream
Coffee, Milk, Tea, Beer, Wine

III. Make a list of all your favorite foods. Then tell your partner about them. Switch roles.

IV. Make a list of the foods you don't like, and use the following language to talk about them:

I don't like it because it tastes . . .
The first time I ate it I . . .
Whenever I eat it I always . . .
The worst thing about it is . . .

Sharing

Waiters and waitresses in good restaurants are often very polite. They use phrases that are not used much in everyday conversation ("would you care for," "may I take your order"). In English, there is no special formula for starting a meal. The French say bon appétit, but in English-speaking countries, people usually talk about how good the food looks or smells, how hungry they are, or what a good job the cook has done preparing the food.

I. At the beginning of a meal in your country, do people do or say anything special? Can you think of any interesting customs involving meals or food and drink in your country or elsewhere?

II. What is your favorite dish? What's in it? How do you make it? What's the best meal you have ever had? Describe it. What is the strangest food you have ever eaten? Name your favorite restaurant and talk about it.

III. What do you think about diets? Do you know someone who has dieted? Have you? What is the purpose of dieting? Do you think women diet more than men? Do you think that women diet to please men? What do you do if the service is bad in a restaurant? How do you feel about tipping? How much does it usually cost to eat out?

Try Your Hand

Study the following menu and then write on the topics below.

Café Formidable
French Onion Soup

(Choose One)
Sirloin Steak
Roast Beef
Seafood Special

Green Salad

Chocolate Mousse

Coffee or Tea

$20.00

Topic One
Write a letter to Café Formidable commenting on the food and service.

Topic Two
Write out a menu which includes all of your favorite foods and beverages.

Topic Three
Write your parents or friends a letter about your dinner at Café Formidable.

19 | *Why don't you come over?*

Conversation

Tom: Why don't you come over next Saturday, Mayumi?

Mike and I are having a Christmas party at our place.

Mayumi: Thanks, I'd love to. Can I bring anything?

Tom: Sure, that would be fine. What did you have in mind?

Mayumi: What about bringing something to drink?

Tom: That sounds good.

Mayumi: O. K. What if I bring some wine? How's that?

Tom: That would be great!

Mayumi: On second thought, since it's a special occasion,

why don't I bring some champagne?

Tom: Oh Mayumi, you really shouldn't.

Mayumi: Oh please! It's my pleasure.

Tom: That'll be a real treat. We're going to

have lots of good food, and all

your friends will be there.

Mayumi: Thanks for the invitation, Tom.

I'm looking forward to the party.

Tom: See you there. Take care.

Mayumi: Bye now.

Variations

What did you have in mind?
> *who*
> *where*
> *what sort of place*
> *how many people*

What about *bringing something to drink?*
> *calling Betty*
> *going swimming tomorrow*
> *watching television later*
> *playing some good CD's*

What if I *bring some wine?*
> *bake a cake*
> *pick up some beer*
> *come with Pedro*
> *call you on Thursday*

On second thought, *why don't I bring champagne?*
> *let's have coffee*
> *why don't we ask Joanne*
> *I'm not sure what to do*
> *tell her to bring some cookies*

Oh please! **It's my pleasure.**
> *I don't mind at all*
> *not at all*
> *don't worry*
> *that's O. K.*

I'm looking forward to *the party.*
> *your wedding*
> *going to Nepal*
> *the ballet*
> *skiing in the Alps*

Your Turn

I. With your partner, plan a party. Decide what kind of party you want to have. Then decide the time, place, what kind of refreshments (food and drinks) you will serve. Then make an invitation list. Invite anybody you want to: your friends, your favorite singer, author, movie star, disc jockey. Maybe even your English teacher! Take notes and, after you finish, be prepared to tell others about your party.

II. Now invite several people to your party. Suggested language:

A: I'd like to invite you to . . . .
B: Thanks, I'd love to come.

A: Would you like to come over . . . ?
B: Sure, I'd love to.

A: Why don't you come to . . . ?
B: O. K. I'll be there. That sounds like fun.

III. You have accepted an invitation to a party, but something has come up and you will not be able to attend. Let your partner be the host who invited you. Tell him you are sorry that you won't be able to come. Suggested language:

You: *I'm really sorry, but something has come up . . . .*
       I won't be able to make it to your party because . . . .
Host: *We'll miss you.*
       I'm sorry you won't be able to come.

IV. Your partner is giving a party and invites you. You offer to bring something, but she or he hesitates and is not sure whether to accept. Here are some ideas about what to bring:

a cake
beer
guacamole
some videos
potato chips
cheese and crackers
caviar
some music
mineral water

Sharing

Relaxation and free time are as essential as work or study, particularly in today's world where there is so much stress. In many places, young people date in couples. In other places, they go out in groups. Adults often spend time together in cafés or bars. Dancing is another activity that has universal appeal, from the tribal ceremonies of African and Polynesian civilizations to the modern rituals of the ballroom and the disco. For better or worse, however, television has become the primary source of entertainment in most countries.

I. What do people do in your native country for entertainment? Do people go out to dinner a lot? What are the cafés and restaurants like? Do people have parties in their homes?

II. How do you spend your free time? Do you go to movie theaters? Watch videos at home? Play sports? How do you and your friends amuse yourselves when you are together?

III. Some critics have said that television is destroying social life and reducing us all to a vegetable state. In America, the term "couch potato" describes a person who does nothing but stay at home and watch "the tube." Do you think television is having a bad influence on social life in the world? Is television having any positive effects on modern life?

Try Your Hand

Read the following invitation and then write on the topics below.

Leopoldo Bombasto
The Ambassador of Titania

requests the honor of your presence at a
Reception
and
Dinner
in honor of Her Majesty
Princess Lalapalooza
at
The Royal Titanian Embassy
Sunday Evening
July the Twenty-Third
Seven P. M.

Black Tie   *R. S. V. P.*

Topic One
Write a note accepting this invitation.

Topic Two
Write a short note saying that you regret you can't attend the reception.

Topic Three
Write an invitation to a more casual party which you are giving.

20 *What's your favorite holiday?*

Conversation

Tom: Merry Christmas and a Happy New Year, everybody!

Mayumi: Thanks, Tom, I'm really enjoying this party. How about you, Pedro?

Pedro: I am, too. I was starving, but I ate so much that I'm stuffed now.

Tom: What did you like best, Pedro?

Pedro: Hmm. That's hard to say. The fruit cake was delicious, and so were the cookies, but I liked the eggnog best. What about you, Mike?

Mike: I guess I prefer the punch to the eggnog.

Mayumi: The Christmas season is so exciting. What's your favorite holiday, Betty?

Betty: When I was little I used to like Christmas and Easter. But now I prefer Halloween. It's a lot of fun, especially the costume parties. How about you, Pedro?

Pedro: That's easy. I'd rather eat. My favorite is Thanksgiving. There's so much good food.

Variations

The fruit cake was delicious, and so *were the cookies.*
> *was the eggnog*
> *were the walnuts*
> *was the turkey*
> *were the chocolates*

What's your favorite *holiday?*
> *food*
> *kind of music*
> *place to relax*
> *book*

I used to like *Christmas.* But now I prefer *Halloween.*
> *Easter . . . Thanksgiving*
> *New Year's . . . Ramadan*
> *Hanukkah . . . Rosh Hashanah*
> *Boxing Day . . . Christmas*

I like *Halloween,* especially *the costume parties.*
> *Christmas . . . the presents*
> *New York . . . the museums*
> *Cologne . . . the cathedral*
> *India . . . the Taj Mahal*

How about you, **Pedro?**
> *what about you*
> *and you*
> *how do you feel about that*
> *what do you think*

I'd rather *eat.*
> *go disco dancing*
> *sleep*
> *talk about it now*
> *wait till tomorrow*

Your Turn

I.   We all go through changes in life. What did you used to do that you don't do now? How about your tastes in music, literature, sports, games, food, travel? Have there been any changes in the way you spend your free time? Suggested topics:

free time	*teachers*
friends	*dating*
vacations	*music*
school	*movies*
clothes	*sports*

Suggested language:

I used to . . . but now I . . . .
I used to like . . . but now I like . . . .
At one time I was fond of . . . but now I . . . .
A long time ago, I used to like . . . but now . . . .

II. You want to give a present to one of your classmates, but you are not sure what he or she would like. Find out the person's likes and dislikes by having a casual conversation. Try not to let them know you are giving them a present.

III. Make a list of pairs of things and then ask your partner about preferences. Here are a few suggestions to get you started:

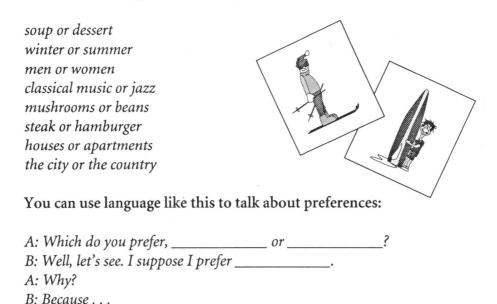

soup or dessert
winter or summer
men or women
classical music or jazz
mushrooms or beans
steak or hamburger
houses or apartments
the city or the country

You can use language like this to talk about preferences:

A: Which do you prefer, _____ or _____?
B: Well, let's see. I suppose I prefer _____.
A: Why?
B: Because . . .

Sharing

Holidays often have their origins in ancient festivals related to religion and agriculture. Every country has such rituals and celebrations to mark important cultural or historic events. Sometimes a religious holiday can lose some of its original meaning and become a secular celebration. Christmas is a good example. Originally it was a Christian holiday on the birthday of Christ, but now it has also become an occasion for parties and gift-giving.

I. What are the chief holidays in your culture? What is the history of these holidays? What is their present meaning? What do people do on these holidays? Are special foods eaten?

II. Tell your classmates about the holiday you like best and why. What kind of holiday is it? Have you had any strange or unusual experiences on this holiday? Any enjoyable ones? Unforgettable ones?

III. Are there any truly international holidays or celebrations which take place all over the world at the same time? What do you think about the Olympic Games held every four years? Are they similar to an international festival? How? Do regional holidays isolate people and prevent internationalization or are they still important?

Try Your Hand

Read the following card and then write on the topics below.

Season's Greetings
Best Wishes
to
You and Yours
for the
Holiday Season

Tom and Mike

Topic One
Explain your favorite holiday to a friend from abroad.

Topic Two
Send your friend a gift and enclose a short note.

Topic Three
Write about your favorite holiday customs.

William Boletta is Professor, Department of English and American Literature, Senshu University, Tokyo. He has taught foreign languages at Duke University and the University of Virginia. Since 1985, he has been teaching English as a foreign language in Japan.